MW00834456

CLASSROOM MANAGEMENT
FOR SCHOOL LIBRARIANS

ALA Editions purchases fund advocacy, awareness, and accreditation programs for library professionals worldwide.

CLASSROOM MANAGEMENT FOR SCHOOL LIBRARIANS

HILDA K. WEISBURG

FOREWORD BY
GAIL K. DICKINSON

ALA
Editions
CHICAGO   2020

HILDA K. WEISBURG was a school librarian for more than thirty years and is now an author, speaker, and adjunct instructor at William Paterson University. She co-authored fourteen books for school librarians (with Ruth Toor), several of which were published by ALA Editions. These include *Being Indispensable: A School Librarian's Guide to Becoming an Invaluable Leader* (2011) and *New on the Job: A School Library Media Specialist's Guide to Success* (2007); in 2013, she published *The School Librarian's Career Planner*, which was her first work without Ruth (who has fully retired). Hilda has since authored a second edition of New on the Job (2014), which has been an ALA best-seller since its 2007 publication. For thirty-five years she co-wrote and edited *School Librarian's Workshop*, a bimonthly newsletter for K–12 librarians. She has given presentations at ALA, AASL, and state library conferences and presented staff development workshops in many locations. A past president of the New Jersey Association of School Librarians, she is a past chair of the AASL Advocacy committee, chairs the Ruth Toor Grant for Strong Public Libraries, and serves on ALA committees. Hilda was the recipient of AASL's 2016 Distinguished Service Award.

© 2020 by Hilda K. Weisburg

Extensive effort has gone into ensuring the reliability of the information in this book; however, the publisher makes no warranty, express or implied, with respect to the material contained herein.

ISBN: 978-0-8389-4804-0 (paper)

Library of Congress Cataloging-in-Publication Data
Names: Weisburg, Hilda K., 1942- author.
Title: Classroom management for school librarians / Hilda K. Weisburg ; foreword by Gail K. Dickinson.
Description: Chicago : ALA Editions, 2020. | Includes bibliographical references and index. | Summary: "This book helps school librarians establish a positive classroom environment and engage students when communicating with and teaching K-12 students"— Provided by publisher.
Identifiers: LCCN 2020015766 | ISBN 9780838948040 (paperback)
Subjects: LCSH: School librarians—United States. | School libraries—United States. | School librarian participation in curriculum planning—United States. | Classroom management—United States. | School librarian-student relationships—United States.
Classification: LCC Z682.4.S34 W447 2020 | DDC 027.80973—dc23
LC record available at https://lccn.loc.gov/2020015766

Cover design by Kim Thornton. Images © Adobe Stock.
Text design in the Chaparral, Gotham, and Bell Gothic typefaces.

♾ This paper meets the requirements of ANSI/NISO Z39.48-1992 (Permanence of Paper).

Printed in the United States of America
24 23 22 21 20   5 4 3 2 1

Contents

GAIL K. DICKINSON

Foreword

I am honored to write the foreword to this book. Managing the enterprise of the school library is one of the most important challenges for school librarians, yet the topic is buried in discussions of other subjects and when it is addressed, the focus is solely on classroom management during the design and delivery of instruction. In the decades since I started my first professional position, libraries have become larger and more complex, and the importance of developing an open and accessible culture in the library remains crucial. Hilda Weisburg and I have discussed this topic many times. Winning the trust of principals and classroom teachers often depends not on the quality of the resources or the innovativeness of the services but rather on the relationships that school librarians build with their communities. As one who has been involved in the school library community at many levels, I believe that this book on managing those relationships—and most importantly, relationships with students—is long overdue.

No matter how long a beginning school librarian has taught in the classroom, no matter how skilled a classroom teacher they were, it's different in the library. Classroom teachers make plans for the group of students they know they will have. They have schedules and structures. School librarians can only guess who will walk in the door—will it be a student or a teacher?

They don't know about the next question they will be asked or the next topic they will be researching. Great school librarians truly see the students not as topics, grade levels, or assignments, but rather as individuals whom they have come to know over a series of grade levels and subject areas. School librarians should be the first people asked to participate in child study teams, because the picture they see is not the same one classroom teachers see.

As Hilda discusses in the first few chapters, sometimes the students are not the only ones who will need some focused classroom management strategies. Most school librarians must manage both the behaviors and the expectations of their peer teachers. Look closely at chapters 3 and 4 for good strategies for working with peer classroom teachers to exploit the resources and services of the school library.

For both students and teachers, a major contributor to negative actions is boredom. Active students will always find something to do, be it positive or negative. And, as noted in chapter 6, sometimes students are defiant. Great school librarians make the library a place where students can explore, are intrigued, and can lose themselves in tasks. As Hilda notes, emergency plans are key for stabilizing inflammatory situations. We cannot control everything that happens in the library or what students have experienced before they walk in the door. We can only address the outcomes of their behavior.

This book will be at the side of school librarians as they seek to build resources and services for all students.

Introduction

When I first conceived of this book, I was thinking of the pre-service school librarians I teach. In my experience, they are eager to learn but may not recognize the special challenges that come with managing the school library classroom. The preponderance of them are classroom teachers who are moving into new roles as school librarians. They believe they know how to manage a classroom. But what they will do in the library classroom is different and far more complex than what they've done in the classroom.

As I discussed this book with other librarians, they eagerly seized on the topic. It was soon apparent that this book was not written just for new librarians, but for all school librarians. Those of you who have been librarians for years will be familiar with much of what will be discussed, but there will be ideas and techniques that will be new to you.

You may recognize some ideas from *Leading for School Librarians: There Is No Other Option* (2017), but in that book I focused on how librarians can become leaders.[1] In *Classroom Management for School Librarians,* the emphasis is on managing your environment. Its premise is that your library is your classroom, and you are responsible for everything that happens there.

MENTORS

As a school librarian, you are expected to know everything there is to know about running and managing a school library program. Yet the people who expect that have little or no idea what your full responsibilities are. A new teacher is not expected to be able to hit the ground running. Their grade level or subject area colleagues can help. That is not true for school librarians.

Only another librarian can understand your situation and challenges, but in most schools you will be the only librarian in the building. If you are new to the profession, seek out a mentor. If you are experienced, find a buddy. You need someone who can be a guide or a listener.

If you are certified through an alternate route that allows you to teach without going through the standard four-year course, you may be assigned a mentor, usually a teacher in your school. This person may be helpful in navigating school procedures but is not a librarian. In this case, you'll need two mentors.

The purpose of a mentor is to guide you as you grow into your full role as a school librarian. Determine which means of communication your mentor prefers and do your best to accommodate it. Be mindful of—and grateful for—your mentor's time.

See if your state library association has a mentorship program and take advantage of it. If not, you must find your own mentor. Consider officers in your state's library association or those who contribute regularly to the association's electronic discussion list or social media platforms. Reach out to one of them. You may think they are too busy or too important to mentor you, but you will be amazed to discover what a helpful, supportive profession this is.

YOUR PHILOSOPHY

Your philosophy, mission, and vision make up a three-legged stool that forms a firm support for your program. You may have some of this in your head, but you need to have them in written form for yourself and others.

Begin by formulating your philosophy. There are numerous titles for what we do. We are called school librarians, teacher librarians, and school library media specialists. The name is not important. What is important is who you are and what you stand for. Knowing this keeps you confident and focused as you manage your shifting roles and responsibilities.

Begin by identifying your core values. What do you think is most important and vital to a school library program? A good place to start is the following six Common Beliefs in the *National School Library Standards for Learners, School Librarians, and School Libraries*:[2]

1. The school library is a unique and essential part of a learning community.
2. Qualified school librarians lead effective school libraries.
3. Learners should be prepared for college, career, and life.
4. Reading is the core of personal and academic competency.
5. Intellectual freedom is every learner's right.
6. Information technologies must be appropriately integrated and equitably available.

Which of these stand out for you? What would you add to your personal list? You need to be clear in your mind about what you believe the library is and what you want it to become. Jot down your thoughts and use them to write your own philosophy statement. You can include what the library should be as well as what the librarian brings to the program.

The completed philosophy statement should be somewhere between two paragraphs and one full page. Because it will be too long to post and share with those who come to the library, use one of the word cloud apps to create a picture of your philosophy and hang that in a prominent place in the library.

YOUR MISSION

Every librarian needs to have both a mission statement and a vision statement, posted where all can see them. As the second leg of that three-legged stool, your mission statement declares your purpose. Why are you here? What makes you indispensable to the school community?

Your philosophy is your foundation. Your mission is your motivation— and your perspiration. It's why you do what you do. You should be proud every time you see it.

I have discussed writing your philosophy statement as well as your vision statement in my earlier books. I hope you already have written one, but it's always good to review your mission statement and see if it needs any tweaks. Write it in the present tense. It's not about what you will do in the future. It's about what you are doing now. Don't use the conditional tense. Again, it's not about what you should do, it's what you're doing. Don't minimize it.

I have seen long mission statements that include bulleted statements detailing how the mission will be realized. I prefer to limit the statement to no more than fifty words. This allows it to be easily framed and hung—and you can memorize it. When you know your mission statement by heart, it stays with you all the time.

Your mission statement promotes the library program as essential. It shows that the library is unique and can't be replaced by anything or anyone. If some other teacher in the school covers what you have included, you are redundant.

Avoid weak words. Saying you *support, extend,* or *complement* the curriculum is nice, but in tough times the administration can do without it. Being *integral* to achieving curricular goals is more powerful.

You will find many examples of mission statements in my earlier book, *Leading for School Librarians.*[3] Here are another two examples to consider:

> The mission of the school library program is to achieve district and curricular goals, address diverse learning and teaching styles of students and faculty, enabling them to become effective users and producers of information by providing them with the technology, resources and guidance they need to stay informed in a rapidly changing world and thrive in a collaborative and productive environment.

> The Library Media Program teaches effective and ethical uses of information, develops critical thinking, fosters and promotes independent reading, provides equitably accessible media sources to all users, and builds personal and social responsibility.

If you are trying to reach your administrators through your mission statement, choose words and terms that are part of their vocabulary. For example, in the last example the phrase "independent reading" is used. But administrators are more concerned with literacy. Instead say, "fosters and promotes literacy through independent reading."

Before deciding that your mission statement is complete, review your school and any district goals. Does it include words that you could include in your statement? Aligning your mission statement with the larger school or district goals demonstrates that you are an integral part of the educational community, and that what you do furthers their aims.

In addition to informing others about the unique and vital role of the library program and educating them about your role, the mission statement will help you to focus your own decision-making It's your touchstone for determining where you want to go, whether to introduce a new program, and who to target for your advocacy. As much as possible all your work should be related to carrying out your mission.

YOUR VISION

Your vision statement is the third leg of the stool. It represents your aspirations and inspirations. It captures an exciting view of what the library program can offer.

Your vision statement shows what your library program would be like in the best of all possible worlds. How do you want others to perceive you? What do you ultimately want to achieve? What messages should the library send?

Even if there's an existing vision statement (and if you do have one, you'll probably need to revise it), make sure it's written in the present tense. This gives it immediacy. Keep it to no more than fifty words so it, too, can be memorized, framed, and hung on your library wall.

Writing a vision statement is more challenging than writing a mission statement. It's hard to reach for something you believe is unattainable, but if you don't put it out there's absolutely no chance that it will be realized.

Leading for School Librarians gives sample vision statements for you to work with, but here are three more examples:[4]

> The Blank School Library Media Program is the center of collaborative learning producing creative students who have an appreciation of literature, critical thinking skills, and a respect for others and self, and who are prepared to make a contribution to the world.

> The school library media program is a safe, open, accessible and inviting learning library commons, essential to student achievement, citizenship and support the principles of intellectual freedom. Our students think globally and are capable of creating new knowledge.

> The Blank Elementary School Library Media Center is the hub for educational resources utilized by students and staff members. With literacy as its core, our Library Media Program stimulates curiosity, innovation, and the skills and techniques forming the foundation for lifetime learning.

Review your vision statement at the start of every school year. Have you taken any steps towards achieving it? What could you try this year that will bring you closer? Consider applying for grants that might fund your efforts.

Whether you're a new or an experienced librarian, you are now ready to explore the challenges of classroom management in the library setting. You will never be bored. Every day will be different. Whether you are at the elementary, middle, or high school level, you will learn something new each day. The demands are many, but the rewards are greater.

NOTES

1. Hilda K. Weisburg, *Leading for School Librarians: There Is No Other Option* (Chicago: Neal-Schuman, 2017).
2. American Association of School Libraries, *National School Library Standards for Learners, School Librarians, and School Libraries,* 2018, 11–14.
3. Weisburg, *Leading for School Librarians,* 14–18.
4. Weisburg, *Leading for School Librarians,* 21.

1

The Library Classroom—
It's Different

Why do school librarians need a book on classroom management targeted specifically to them? A classroom is a classroom. Teaching is teaching. Both are true—and yet far from the truth. Those of you who are classroom teachers have been working with students for some time. If you are new to education, of course, you would want to learn about this. But why is this book just for school librarians? The reason is that there are many factors, from the physical space to the way you meet with students, that make the library very different from a regular classroom. The library comes with a new set of challenges. For your library program to succeed, you need to become comfortable with these challenges and know how to deal with them.

A classroom is designed to hold about thirty students. Although there may be bookcases for a classroom collection, a cart with computers or Chromebooks, and even some comfortable seating, it is still basically a rectangle that is designed so students will focus on a teacher at the front of the room. A library is far larger. It has more shelves, display areas, and different types of lounge furniture. At the elementary level, there will be a section for story listening A library may have DVDs, magazines, a green wall or possibly a makerspace, as well as other features common in school libraries today. And that's just what the students normally see. There is also usually an office and a workroom area.

In short, it doesn't look anything like a classroom. It encourages exploration which will motivate your students to discover and learn. At the same time, the open space provides opportunities for students to get lost in the stacks, avoid work, and occasionally cause trouble.

Classroom teachers at the elementary level meet with their students every day, all day, except for "specials" such as prep periods and when students go to art, music, and gym classes —and to the library. An elementary librarian may only see students from every grade level once a week for 30 to 45 minutes. In some districts these may be scheduled once every six days or less. Holidays and snow days can stretch out the time between sessions even further. This could be once every six days or even less frequently. Getting to know each student is not easy. Nor is it a simple matter to fit in time for lessons, book selection, checkout, and book returns before the next class arrives.

In middle and high schools, unless you have a special course to teach, you'll have even less frequent contact. You see students when the teachers bring in their classes. You can easily have a senior English class, followed by an ELL class, and then a French II class. Sometimes two or three of these disparate classes will be in the library simultaneously.

Depending on the connections you have made with teachers, students may come in for only a single day for you to introduce the research process, or for several days in a row, perhaps with you and the teacher working together. Sometimes a teacher just brings in a class and doesn't want you to do anything. There is no one set way. It will be different from one teacher to another. How this goes very much depends on how proactive you are and how successfully you develop relationships with teachers.

Regardless of grade level, when classes come into your library you won't be working with your own students. It's hard to get to know them all. At a large middle or high school, it is impossible to do so. Older students recognize this, and some will not acknowledge your authority the way they do with their teachers. Students in upper grades like to find places where they won't be seen. With younger students, it can feel like you're herding cats because they want to spread throughout the library.

MANAGEMENT VERSUS CONTROL

In my previous book, *Leading for School Librarians*, I devoted a chapter to managing classes in the library. It's worth reviewing what was covered there before going into greater detail.[1] What do you do when twenty-five or more students come into your library at once? Whether they are dropped off by elementary teachers or accompanied by middle or high school teachers, they are in your space. You are responsible.

If you are unsure of yourself, your instinctive reaction is to try to control these situations, and that's where you make your first mistake. The title of this book is *Classroom Management for School Librarians*. The keyword is *management*—not control.

The *Merriam-Webster* dictionary defines *control* as "to exercise restraining or dominating influence over" and "to have power over."[2] By contrast, it defines *management* as "to work upon or try to alter for a purpose" and "to succeed in accomplishing."[3] (Note that I carefully chose particular definitions to highlight the difference between the two words.)

Obviously, you want to manage student behavior, not control it. If you are uncertain of what you are doing—if you don't know how to manage students and other challenges when they arise, you move into fight or flight mode, which inevitably means trying to control the situation. Once you do that, you have, in fact, lost control.

Even more than classroom teachers, librarians face more challenges in managing their environment. You need to develop tools to keep you calm and capable of confidently managing your school library.

Think of how you feel when you are thrust into a challenging situation. Can you sense your body tightening or have a sinking feeling in your stomach? Body language communicates even more than words. In the various scenarios that will be discussed, it's the nonverbal communication that must be understood and mastered.

Be mindful of your body's reactions. To dispel the need to control, when you feel that panic, take a few deep breaths (shallow breathing intensifies fear). Have a short phrase that states something you know is true and repeat it in your mind. Draw on your philosophy. As discussed in the introduction, this is the statement of your core values. Do you believe every student can learn? Do you want the library to be a safe, welcoming environment? Your short phrase then might be "I know how to make their learning fun/engaging" or "They are all welcome here."

Feel your shoulders relax as you silently repeat your phrase one or twice. Smile, and mean it. Look students in the eye as you do so. Make a welcoming comment to one or more students as they enter or settle into their places.

You are now managing the situation. The kids will respond to that. We are innately conditioned to trust a leader who is in charge. By contrast, we will drift like a rudderless boat when the leader doesn't seem able to lead. When you know how to manage yourself, you won't need to control. The more you worry about discipline, the less likely you are to have it.

At all levels, you must make connections to the students. The library must be a safe, welcoming space for all. Everything you do must advance that. When interacting with students—and with teachers, administrators, and others—always keep that in mind.

USING YOUR POWER

Do you feel uncomfortable with the idea of using power? What does power mean to you? Many people have a negative reaction to it. They immediately go to the authoritarian use of power, which seems out of place in a school, particularly in a library where you want to create a safe, welcoming—and even nurturing—environment.

Power in and of itself is neither negative nor positive. What matters is how power is used. In *Leading for School Librarians,* I discussed the Five Bases of Social Power proposed by John R. P. French Jr. and Bertram Russell.[4] They defined power as the ability to cause someone to do something and defined five types of power:

- *Legitimate.* The power wielded by a person in authority who has a title such as "principal."
- *Coercive.* The power of someone with the ability to punish.
- *Reward.* The power held by someone who has the ability to reward.
- *Expert.* The power comes from a person who is knowledgeable about something that others need to know.
- *Referent.* The power based on the charisma of a person you to work with.

Teachers and librarians, to varying degrees, have legitimate, coercive, and reward power, which are negative powers. It may seem as though reward power would be positive, but it's the carrot on a stick. The implied threat is if you don't do what the person in authority wants, the reward will be taken away and be replaced by punishment, or coercive power.

The expert and referent powers are more likely to be positive in nature. As a librarian you have a lot of expert power, but this power can be short term. Once the person learns what they need or want to know, the expert power disappears. The most long-term and strongest of the five is referent power. It will come into play in managing the library classroom because it rests on your ability to create and sustain relationships with the educational community.

An understanding of how to use power positively is vital to your success. As the adult in charge of the library, you are the one in power. How you use it sets the tone for your library. There are teachers who use their power to control their students. You undoubtedly have come across a few of them in your own educational experiences. But you don't want control. For one thing, control is contrary to the environment that you must create in your library.

There are multiple ways to look at power beyond what French and Russell defined. PowerCube offers three expressions of power: Power Over, Power Within, and Power With.[5] These are simple to understand and are an excellent explanation of the dynamics in play within a classroom and other settings.

Because almost all social interactions have elements of power intertwined within them, this is another way to look at power undercurrents and to see how to effectively use the positive ones to improve your classroom management and create the library atmosphere you want.

Power Over means using your position to exert control. It is authoritarian in nature. Much like legitimate, coercive, and reward powers, it suppresses initiative, produces resentment, and often results in rebellion. You have seen it in action, possibly experiencing it yourself in your own student days or when interacting with a supervisor.

In a challenging situation, it is almost instinctive to use Power Over, but it will undermine whatever positives you are building. When this happens, and it invariably does, you can minimize the damage by apologizing. Students are not accustomed to adults admitting they made a mistake. When you apologize to students, you are giving them a lesson in how to respond when they slip up.

Power Within is based on trust in yourself. It is rooted in self-confidence. You can feel it inside you as you go through your day. When you love what you do and believe in its value and importance, you can draw on it in your interactions. By definition, it allows you to manage situations. This is where your positive mindset comes from.

When you exude Power Within, others recognize that you are confident, which leads to trust. Trust is a core foundation for relationships, and relationships with students, teachers, and the educational community are vital to your success. Students are far more likely to listen to and follow you when they feel you know what you are doing.

Power With is even stronger. It is an outgrowth of Power Within. When you are confident, you can easily connect with others and draw out their best. When you have Power With, you can engage people to work with you towards a goal. To some extent it is related to referent power. When you interact with teachers, it is Power With that leads to collaboration. When you work with students, it generates trust. If you foster students' Power With you encourage their initiative and curiosity, engaging them in learning that's meaningful to them.

Don't forget that power is always at play in social interactions. This means students are using their power, mostly unknowingly.

CHILDREN'S GROWTH AND DEVELOPMENT

As a librarian you can't be sure about the grade levels you will be teaching. You may envision yourself as an elementary librarian but find yourself in a middle school. Depending on how your degree reads, you may be able to work at all grade levels. And, unlike classroom teachers, you will be dealing with multiple grades no matter the level of your school.

As children progress from kindergarten through high school they go through constant changes in their physical, social, emotional, and cognitive development. It's important to be aware of these changes and the factors that affect students' behavior. The more you recognize what is going on inside their heads and bodies, the better you will be at managing the library classroom.

On its website, the California Department of Education has a page for Ages and Stage of Development, beginning with birth and going through age fourteen.[6] I have drawn from its summary for my discussion below.

K-1

Physically, these children are seemingly always in motion. Their hands and feet never stop. When you set up your expectations you will include something to indicate they should keep their hands and feet to themselves. Even older students need that reminder.

You can't expect students at this age to sit for long periods of time (fifteen minutes is too long) without some type of break. Mentally, they are curious about the world around them. They constantly ask, "Why?" It's important not to squelch their inquisitiveness as it is the basis of all learning. The library is a place of discovery. Allow them opportunities to do so.

Their minds seem to flit from one thought to another. They are masters of the non sequitur. If you ask a question about the story you are reading, one of the students is apt to say something like, "My aunt just had a baby." You can go to Power Over and say, "That's not what we are talking about," or you can use Power With to say, "How exciting," and then repeat your question.

Grades 2-3

By second grade, students are more attuned to school as part of their lives. They are no longer always in motion. Homework becomes important along with how they are doing compared to their peers. They can become easily frustrated, resulting in small or large displays of temper. Be prepared to defuse these situations with supportive solutions. Begin to develop a bag of tricks that work for you and your student population.

Socially, students are becoming more distinct individuals and forming friendships, which also bring arguments. Storytime should be about more than just about the story. You can use it to teach kindness and how to cope with anger and frustration. If you have identified a particular problem students are experiencing when they are dealing with emotions or "failure," find stories that will guide them into understanding how to manage these situations.

As part of the classroom management plan you will create, include a realistic series of consequences to respond to students who are acting out. Start by giving them a quick look to remind them that they are not behaving well or are causing a distraction. Asking a question moves the student from where they are to where they need to be. Eventually, you will have a collection of strategies that will resolve most situations. Chapter 6 goes into more detail on handling disruptions.

Grades 4–6

Behaviors and physical development begin to range more widely. Some children still act like second graders while some fifth and sixth graders are in the early stages of puberty. They are more likely not to accept a rule for its own sake. Be sure they understand the reasons for it.

Children at this age want to be "big." They like feeling grown up and doing things older kids do. If at all possible, this is a great age to begin having student volunteers. They love working in the library and are usually conscientious.

Research projects based on their interests, such as clothing and music, will engage them. Although inquiry-based learning can and should begin at the primary level, these are brief forays. This is when they can begin developing research strategies.

ADOLESCENTS' GROWTH AND DEVELOPMENT

You either love working with adolescents or hate it. Regardless, you need to get a handle on what is going on inside them. The American Psychological Association's *Developing Adolescents: A Resource for Professionals* is another resource you should bookmark and consult as needed.[7]

Working with adolescents can be an exhilarating experience or a mine-field depending on how you view it. Emotions are on display—full out. On the other hand, you can have fun with them. They get the jokes.

You can watch them evolving into the adults they are going to be. The road is not straight and is often fraught with angst. This is an enduring subject of YA fiction and in the creative writing of students. Pecking orders and cliques are common. Long-standing friendships break up over them.

Every day is a new crisis. If you speak to students of this age and treat them as though they are adults, you can develop a positive relationship with them. In turn, they will keep you young.

Grades 7–9

This age range is the most challenging as the span between different kids' emotional and physical age varies widely. While the adults are focused on teaching the curriculum, a stew of young adolescent emotions are stirring below the surface. If you develop relationships with your students, you can tune into what they're feeling and help them with some of the turmoil.

Puberty arrives for most students during the years between eleven and fourteen, although sometimes they still sound and act like six-year-olds. They will experience emotional extremes more frequently. Within hours they can move from life is wonderful to life is a disaster. Don't react to the emotion—focus on the content.

Students of this age become more aware of what's going on in the adult world. They may develop an interest in politics and activism. At the same time, this is an age when bullying (including cyberbullying) become a problem. Mean girls are a well-known segment of middle school students. Boys who are not into sports may be targeted.

Sexuality also becomes an issue. Body and sexual changes often cause concerns, voiced or not. In general, the girls will be ahead of the boys, but you still need to be aware of the interplay between and within the genders. Boys who haven't come into their growth spurt or girls who have not begun menstruating feel "less" than others of their age. Body-shaming is common.

Additionally, there are students who are discovering or suspecting they are LGBTQ+. Even in tolerant communities, being discovered or coming out can be frightening. Being different is not comfortable and sometimes not safe. The role of the library as a safe, welcoming space for all becomes more important than ever. In addition to having books that students can see themselves in, occasionally the library needs to be a place where they can hide. Being able to have lunch in the library has been a sanctuary for many.

Risky behaviors tend to begin in this age range. From smoking and vaping to alcohol and drugs, many tweens, begin to experiment. Not wearing bike helmets during this period transitions into reckless driving when they are old enough to get a driver's license. Add early (and later) sexual experimentation and unsafe social networking practices and you can readily see how volatile this time period can be.

The library is a unique environment and you will see the kids in ways the teachers don't. Be alert to signs of potential trouble. Be the trusted adult, and, if necessary, get them to a counselor. Because you don't want to violate their trust, go to a counselor only as a last resort.

Grades 10–12

Cognitively, high school students are now much better at higher-order thinking skills, but they still need help in thinking critically. Librarians are in a perfect position to guide them by working with teachers to craft projects that require them to learn to assess the validity and relevance of information while creating new knowledge.

All the physical and emotional changes that emerged in middle school continue into high school with the added tension of becoming "college ready." The reality of looming adulthood is both exciting and frightening. Whether they plan to go to college, the military, or enter a career right out of high school, their days as students are coming to an end. The pressure can be intense, and sometimes exacerbated by parents' expectations and demands.

Adolescents are frustrated by adults' failure to treat them as grown-ups. For them, this means being given more freedom. Parents and teachers feel they are treating them as adults by giving them more responsibilities. It is a disconnect that can't be resolved easily and leads to many arguments between parents and kids as well as some clashes between teachers and students.

Given the behavior and emotional extremes of high school students, it can be difficult to determine if a teenager is heading for trouble or is just manifesting an aspect of typical behavior. *Developing Adolescents: A Resource for Professionals* explains it is normal for adolescents to:

- argue for the sake of arguing
- jump to conclusions
- be self-centered
- constantly find fault in adults' positions
- be overly dramatic[8]

Recognize when they are arguing just to do so, and don't get sucked into it. Some of this is bluster coming from their own uncertainties as well as trying to cope with negative self-esteem while simultaneously wanting to appear grown up.

In your role as librarian, you can help them learn not to jump to conclusions. Don't tell them they are wrong. Rather ask them to prove their belief and guide them in their search. A KWL (what I know, what I want to know, what I learned) chart is a simple and effective tool. They may learn that what they thought they knew wasn't true.

Teenagers' insecurities contribute to them becoming self-centered. Everything is about them. The drama is related to this, as well as to the emotional extremes that are a natural part of adolescence.

Teens continue to engage in the risky behaviors that began in middle school. Now that driving is added to the mix along with more time away from adult supervision, there can be more far-reaching consequences. They are testing limits—theirs and yours—and don't always recognize or fear the dangers. It's often said that adolescents have a sense that they are immortal. Additionally, their brains are not fully developed, and they often can't predict the consequences of actions. Adults sometimes ask teenagers, "What were you thinking?" The honest answer is—they weren't.

I have told my grandsons, "If one of your friends says, 'wouldn't it be great to...,' the answer is 'no.'" More seriously, your ability to develop relationships with students will make you one of their trusted adults, allowing you to sometimes avert one of these risky decisions.

When they trust you, students will sometimes talk to you about personal and other matters. *Developing Adolescents: A Resource for Professionals* offers the following advice for talking with adolescents (the direct quotes are in italics; the comments are not):

- *Listen nonjudgmentally (and listen more than you speak).*
  Adolescents really need someone who can listen to them rather
  than talk at them. By listening, you can pluck out the core of the
  issue, which is likely to be embedded somewhere within what
  they are saying.
- *Ask open-ended questions.* This is how you guide students
  into becoming independent thinkers. Your questions should
  encourage them to reflect on their thoughts, words, and actions.
  Consider something like, "What do you think might be the result
  of ....?"
- *Avoid "why" questions*—As noted earlier, they won't often know
  why they did something. You're also challenging them, which can
  cause them to shut down.
- *Match the adolescent's emotional state, unless it is hostile.* You don't
  want to put a damper on their enthusiasm even if you think it
  is misplaced. Nor do you want to negate their feeling of being
  unloved. You start by saying, "I can see how excited (or unhappy)
  you are." From there, you can work with them and try to help
  them explore their feelings and find a more balanced state or
  resolve a problem.
- *Casually model rational decision-making.* Sharing your own
  experiences can be helpful. Remember, students at all ages learn
  more from what we do than what we say. Share your reasoning
  when appropriate.
- *Discuss ethical and moral problems that are in the news.* This
  expands their social consciousness and also treats students as
  adults who have ideas worth sharing. Work with teachers to
  create projects that give them opportunities to wrestle with
  difficult issues they're interested in. It will help them develop
  empathy and minimize their self-centeredness.[9]

The ups and downs of the teen years notwithstanding, you can accomplish much simply by following the suggestions given in Mary Anne Ware and Jodi Rath's "Four Must-Haves for Positive Teacher-Teen Relationships."[10]

Consistency. All students need consistency, but none more than teens, whose lives are always at extremes. Consistency grounds them. It reminds them that they know what will happen next. Consistently applied boundaries helps them avoid risky behaviors.

Respect. Although respect is necessary for all relationships, starting with the youngest children, it becomes increasingly important with teens. If you don't give them respect, they won't give it to you and the likelihood of confrontations increases. Don't stop a conversation with them because an adult wants to speak with you. That sends the message that you don't think they are as important.

High expectations. This is a form of respect. You are acknowledging the student is capable but show your willingness to help them achieve their goal. Dumbing something down is insulting, and they will recognize it.

Kindness. This sounds simple and obvious, but it can easily be overlooked on a busy day. In the words of a wise man, "The world is like a mirror. Smile at it and it will smile back." This works with teens as much as anyone else. I don't think I went through a day when I was a high school librarian when I wasn't thanked at least once by students. And I thanked them often as well.

REFLECTION

The library classroom is obviously not the same as a teacher's classroom, yet it is a classroom. It is where true learning occurs. A parade of students come through its doors and find the help and resources to meet their educational and personal needs.

While they are in that space, they are welcome and safe—safe to explore, discover, and create. The librarian gets to watch and guide students as they grow and develop into the adults they will become.

KEY IDEAS

- The library classroom resembles a teacher's classroom in name only.
- Physically, the library classroom is different from a teacher's classroom, and this affects student behavior.
- At the elementary level, the librarian meets with different grades and students all day, seeing them, at best, once a week.
- At upper levels, librarians are dependent on teachers bringing in their classes, which are at all grades and subject areas.
- The students are not "yours." Within the library classroom, they still belong to their teacher, and they know it.
- You need to manage, not control, your library classroom.
- Control is about dominance; management is about working with people (students in this case).
- When you are fearful you try to exert control.
- Your body language communicates more than your words.
- Have a plan to move your mindset from fearing the situation to managing it.
- All social interactions involve some type of power.
- Power in and of itself is neither negative nor positive.
- Power Over is control, not management.

- Power Within comes from self-confidence.
- Power With enables collaboration to occur.
- Understanding the physical, emotional, and cognitive development stages of children from kindergarten through high school allows you to teach and respond to them in a manner appropriate to the appropriate level.
- Primary grade children become socialized to the school environment, become surer in their individual nature, and build friendships,
- By the elementary grades, some children are beginning to enter puberty while others are still little kids.
- Although elementary students tend to get into difficulties because, at this developmental stage, they are physical, adolescents are challenged by and are challenging because of their emotional extremes.
- Middle school is most challenging because the range in physical and emotional development among students is the greatest.
- Body image is important to teens and body shaming becomes a problem along with bullying and cyberbullying.
- The library as a safe, welcoming space becomes extremely important. Some students will use it as a sanctuary during lunch.
- Risky behavior including smoking, drinking, taking drugs, and having sex begin during these years, and the librarian can and should be a "trusted adult" who can help them.
- High school students can better employ high-order thinking skills but don't always think critically. Well-crafted assignments can help them learn how to do so.
- The imminence of adulthood adds more pressure.
- When dealing with an argumentative, self-absorbed teen, remember that this is normal behavior.
- Develop strategies for talking with teens.
- Remember to listen more than talk, ask questions that require thought, and don't ask "Why?" They have no idea why.
- Be a role model for good decision-making and engage students in what is happening in the world around them.
- In your dealings with teens, be consistent, give and expect respect, hold them to high standards, and show kindness.

NOTES

1. Hilda K. Weisburg, *Leading for School Librarians: There Is No Other Option* (Chicago: Neal-Schuman, 2017), 29–38.
2. Merriam-Webster.com, s.v. "control," https://www.merriam-webster.com/dictionary/control.
3. Merriam-Webster.com, s.v. "manage," https://www.merriam-webster.com/dictionary/manage.
4. Weisburg, *Leading for School Librarians,* 72–73; J. R. P. French, Jr., and B. Raven, "The Bases of Social Power," in *Classics of Organization Theory,* ed. Jay M. Shafritz, J. Steven Ott, and Yong Suk Jang (CENGAGE Learning, 2015), EPUB.
5. "Expressions of Power," PowerCube, https://www.powercube.net/other-forms -of-power/expressions-of-power/.
6. California Department of Education, "Ages and Stages of Development," https://www.cde.ca.gov/sp/cd/re/caqdevelopment.asp.
7. *Developing Adolescents: A Resource for Professionals* (Washington, DC: American Psychological Association, 2002), https://www.apa.org/pi/families/resources/develop.pdf.
8. *Developing Adolescents.*
9. *Developing Adolescents*, 11.
10. M. A. Ware and Jodi Rath, "Four Must-Haves for Positive Teacher-Teen Relationships," *ASCD Express* 14, no. 26 (2019), www.ascd.org/ascd-express/vol14/num26/4-must-haves-for-positive-teacher-teen-relationships.aspx.

2
Begin as You Mean to Go On

How you begin sets the tone for the rest of the school year. It's always harder to fix something than to get it right the first time. Not that you won't make errors—it's a part of your continuous learning, but the better you can prepare and anticipate what is coming, the fewer times you will need to change course. In the words of Charles H. Spurgeon, "Begin as you mean to go on, and go on as you began."[1]

Although your teaching space may be in one section of the library, particularly if you are in an elementary school, in reality, your library classroom is the entire library. How it looks and feels sends a message to students and anyone else who comes in. Take a critical look at it from the perspective of someone seeing it for the first time to determine what it is communicating.

Many adults who have recounted their memories of their time in school remember that the library was the one place they felt safe. It also should be a pressure-free space. For teachers as well as students, the school library needs to be a welcoming haven. The library you take over may or may not be that space. If it isn't, it is up to you to change it.

ASSESSING YOUR FACILITY

The first step in creating a safe, welcoming environment is to assess your facility. It can work for or against you. Obviously, a library and a classroom look very different. The desks, whatever their configuration, send a signal about work and learning. Although the library classroom is also about learning, the emphasis is on promoting exploration and discovery. The resources available for this are varied; nonetheless, the furniture and design should reflect the different ways they will be used.

Furniture and Shelving

Furniture should reflect the age and needs of the users. You will see less wriggling or leaning back on chairs if their design is age appropriate. Note that round tables are best for promoting collaboration. If you have the opportunity to purchase tables and chairs, choose ones with casters so that table arrangements can be quickly reconfigured, and chairs moved easily. The custodial staff will love you for it.

Elementary libraries need a space for students to listen to stories. Books should not be on shelves that are too high for them to reach. If you have tall bookcases, use the top shelves for displays. Bean bags are often used at the elementary level and various lounge chairs are common at the middle and high school levels. Displaying student work also adds a welcoming note.

Look online for pictures of school libraries at your grade level. Which ones appeal to you? Can you create a similar environment without spending much or any money? If you have been at your school for a few years, you can propose a refurbishing. Look for grants and possibly online sources such as DonorsChoose to raise the necessary funds. Of course, a capital line in the budget would be best, but that is hard to get.

In many libraries there are numerous places where students can hide. You want to be able to view what is happening everywhere. In the ideal situation, tall bookcases would only be positioned against the walls. Counter-height bookstacks break up the space but are easy to see over. When possible, these low bookstacks should have casters that allow you to change the configuration of the space as needed.

If there are blind spots, try to purchase security mirrors. In addition to the usual approach of going to Amazon, check library supply houses such as Demco (www.demco.com), Brodart (www.brodart.com), and The Library Store (www.thelibrarystore.com). You should become acquainted with what you can purchase from these and similar sources.

Where possible, set up an area for teachers. Professional magazines can be kept here as well as any professional literature you have. Making teachers feel welcome and valued lays the foundation for collaboration.

Signage

When you go to an airport or the supermarket, you count on signs to help you navigate the space. Your library needs to help users find what they want with the least possible confusion. Clear signage is extremely important, as is the wording you use for them. "Checkout" is more easily understood than "Circulation Desk." "Information" or "Questions?" are better alternatives than "Reference."

Consider facing books outward so the covers can be seen. Some libraries have end caps that they use for this. You can't arrange all books that way but choosing a few can be a lure for students. Bins are good for pictures books because students can see the covers as they flip through them.

You also need signs identifying the different sections of the book collection. For almost 150 years, public and then school libraries have been arranging nonfiction by the Dewey Decimal System. Although that is still predominantly true, many librarians have chosen to genrify their collection. This is particularly true in elementary libraries where students may have trouble dealing with the decimals. Many librarians have only genrefied fiction rather than arranging all the books alphabetically by author.

Your decision as to the classification system you use should be based on what is best for your users. Whichever you choose, signage is critical. Pictures indicating what can be found in the sections are extremely helpful. Hang posters showing all the Dewey or genre categories.

Series books are popular from the elementary grades on up. They can be shelved separately if that works best with your students. Number them in sequence rather than putting them in alphabetical order by title.

Displays

Bulletin boards and displays ignite interest. They need to be changed regularly. I knew one librarian who put up their bulletin board when school opened and didn't change it for the entire year. As you can guess students and teachers stopped seeing it after two months.

You might use one bulletin board to feature a special month, from National Hispanic Heritage Month (September 15–October 15) to National Safety Month in June. You can always invent a theme for a month if needed. Bulletin boards take time to do but are worth the effort as they also make the library more attractive.

Interactive bulletin boards draw student attention and support engagement. One good way to promote interest is to create a board on which they can post questions concerning things they are curious about or share something about a book they're reading. You can use them as de-stressors by putting up a large coloring page for students to work on. You can focus them on social and emotional learning (SEL) by asking them to share what they are thankful for or give examples of ways they show or have received kindness. Pinterest has many ideas you can use.

Use display cases to feature new books or a selection on a topic of interest. Search online and you'll find numerous ways to create library displays. Choose those you like. You can also enlist others, such as library volunteers or art students, to help if you are artistically challenged.

Student work is the best thing to display. Putting students in the spotlight encourages their efforts. Also feature individual and team accomplishments. Although sports achievements are common, don't forget academic teams. You can find many ideas to duplicate, adapt, or spur your own creativity on Pinterest, Instagram, and the various Facebook groups on school libraries.

Also consider plants. They do well in libraries and create a welcoming atmosphere. If you don't have a green thumb, look for easy-to-maintain plants, or you might find someone who would love to tend to them. Place some books on flowers and gardening next to them.

Automated Systems

Your automated library system (ALS) is one of the first things to explore. Even today, there are still schools that don't have an ALS. If so, you need to plan how you will acquire an automated system for your library. Students will be using an online public access computer (OPAC) in every library they go to. It will hinder their learning if they don't have access to one in school. You need one to prepare students for their future—and even for everyday life.

If the system is new to you, contact the vendor to learn about the basics. Right from the start you will need to input new students and teachers into the system and check books in and out almost immediately. Your vendor should supply you with tutorials to help.

As stated in the opening of this chapter, begin as you mean to go on. With your circulation system, you usually need to plan for the end of the year at the very beginning of the school year. Check with your vendor if you need to learn how to set a final date to check books out. Hopefully, this will be two or three weeks before the school year ends. The time cushion allows for an orderly closing Before you lock in the dates, confirm your plan with your principal. Informing the principal about these dates is important because they might want to shorten that time. It could be you are not seeing the larger constraints the administration faces. Explain your reasons but do what you are told.

ORIENTATIONS

Students usually meet you for the first time when they come to the library for orientation. As the saying goes, you have only one chance to make a first impression. Elementary students typically get "oriented" each year. Middle and high school students have an orientation in the year they enter, usually this is with their ELA or social studies teacher.

Students will be assessing you during this time and determining whether they like you. You want them to see you as helpful, approachable, and friendly. You are their guide to the explorations they will be doing academically and personally.

In addition to seeing the library as a safe, welcoming space, students should view it as a place where they can discover ideas and information for their school and personal needs. At the elementary level, this may mean that in addition to books they will be exploring interesting websites and apps or creating in a makerspace. For middle and high school students, books are still important but so are databases and other resources you may have such as a green wall or screen for filming or a Lego wall.

The orientation sets the tone for the rest of the school year. Consider what you want to achieve and make it interesting. You want students to enjoy the library, but fun isn't its only purpose. What do you want students to take away?

Once you know your purpose, you can design the orientation. Do you just want students to know where materials are located? Your signage should be good enough to answer those questions. Your displays will make it easy for even kindergartners to find books. Students can learn the procedure for checking out when they have selected their book. We learn better by doing than by listening.

A scavenger hunts is a common way of making orientation fun, but it's the means, not the goal. What do you want students to find? How will it contribute to your purpose? Search the internet for ideas you can adapt or adopt. Ideally, you can tie the orientation to a mini research project, so they can learn as they go and immediately put what you're teaching into practice.

As you smile and greet students, remember that your body language will reflect your attitude. If you are feeling uncertain, students will know and take advantage of you. Keep a phrase such as, "I've got this!" in your head. Your body will mimic your thoughts.

Your tone of voice also sends a message. Although you don't want to sound authoritarian, you do want to communicate that you are in charge. Send the message that you are welcoming, but you aren't a pushover.

Begin the orientation by asking for input from students. Have any of the kindergartners been to a public library? Start the conversation by asking what they know about libraries. In the process you will discover how much experience they have had. You can use the same questions with older elementary students. Their answers will let you know how they feel about the library as well as what they have learned.

With middle and high school students, have them share what they think are the best—and worst—things about libraries. In addition to focusing the activity, this gives you information and shows students you care about what they think and feel. If they don't like something, have them suggest what can be done differently. Talk about some of the things you plan on doing during the school year. Let them know you are open to suggestions.

Here are some good opening questions that can be tweaked to use at all grade levels:

- What do you want to learn this year?
- If you could go anywhere in the world, where would you go? Why?
- Who is someone you admire? Who do you think is a hero? Why?
- What do you think is the hardest job in the world?

Terry Heick suggests twelve questions to ask your students on the first day of school.[2] Choose the ones most appropriate to your grade levels. They will set the stage for making students feel the library is a safe, welcoming space.

RULES

Some of the feedback you are bound to get to your questions about libraries will be about "the rules." Students may think that librarians want them to be quiet. Although noise levels vary depending on how the librarian chooses to manage the library, silence is never desirable except when listening to a story or being given directions. This should be a relatively short period of time—never an extended silence.

Overall, libraries are not quiet. Too much is happening there for it be silent. This doesn't mean there aren't rules. Elementary librarians often post their rules. Librarians in upper grades may do so as well. However, the rules you choose will add to or detract from the library atmosphere. If you're not careful, they can counter your efforts to make the library a safe, welcoming environment.

I was consulting on a district library program and went into one elementary library in the summer. As soon as I entered, I saw a big poster titled "THE RULES." It was a list of "no's." No loud voices. No running. No pushing while on line. No eating. No writing in the books. No touching other people. Obviously, you don't want to encourage those behaviors, but this wasn't a welcoming way to present them. I was an adult and I wanted to leave!

Instead of rules, think of these as expectations. They need to be stated positively to create the environment you want. My favorite elementary rules are

- Respect yourself.
- Respect others.
- Respect the library.

Post them and discuss what they mean with elementary students. What does "respect yourself" mean? How do you "respect others" in the library? This is when you can explain why they need their hands and feet to themselves and that they shouldn't run in the library. Why and how do you "respect the library?" Introduce the concept of consequences by asking them what they think should happen if they don't do any of these things? (Note that students' suggestions of consequences are often harsher than what you would like.)

Pinterest is a treasure trove of rules. It also has a lot of rules you wouldn't want in your library. Because Pinterest uses images, you might find additional ideas about how to present your expectations. Among some of the excellent expectations you may find are:

- Ask lots of questions.
- Be responsible.
- Take care of books.
- Be kind.
- Learn something new.

Middle school librarians vary about whether they post rules. Use something like SlideShare or another presentation method to introduce and go over your expectations during orientation. Discuss why they are important. Should anything be added? Should adults behave the same way?

Ask high school students to name some library rules. They have been through many orientations since elementary school and think they know everything. When you go over rules, they will tune you out. On the other hand, they are familiar with library behavior. Give then the opportunity to tell you what they believe is appropriate. Some may say, "No talking," thinking that's what you want to hear. Let them know you expect talking and trust they will turn it down if you tell them they are getting too loud.

Whether or not you post them, discuss the expectations. Do students think any more are needed? Which ones? Why?

This type of interchange sets up the connection you need to make with students. It shows you are approachable, that you seek their input, and respect them as people. Tell them they obviously know how to behave in a school library, so if you speak to them about their behavior, they can't tell you they didn't know.

Food

Along with noise, food is an open question. Like standards for how much noise is too much, the question of allowing kids to eat in the library has no clear-cut answers. It used to be simple: food and drink were not permitted.

Students observed meetings in the library when adults ate and drink. Librarians acknowledged that it was the adults who were responsible for most of the carpet stains. Then public libraries began opening cafes.

Enforcing the no food or drink rule was always difficult when students used the library during lunch. Some wanted to get work done and others wanted to socialize with friends and didn't want to waste time in the cafeteria, so they snuck their food in and hoped they didn't get caught. Inevitably librarians found the remains on shelves and in various nooks and crannies. Occasionally a secreted drink would get knocked over as a kid tried to conceal it from an advancing librarian.

Today, librarians have different ideas about what should be allowed. When food is permitted, students are expected to clean up after themselves. They are to keep drinks from computer areas. They shouldn't read with greasy fingers. Some high school libraries have gone so far as to set up coffee bars, but that is still rare.

Whether you allow food and drink depends on what has been acceptable before and how new you are to the school. This kind of change shouldn't be instituted too quickly. You need to know who will disapprove. It's not just the administration. The custodial staff have to be on board as well.

If food is allowed, let them know if they leave garbage behind, they will not be permitted to come during lunch for a set period of time. Putting a garbage can near the exit can remind them.

Food—yes or no? The choice is yours. Make your decision based on your philosophy, mission, and vision. And be sure to get input from teachers and administrators, too.

Cleanliness

It can be hard to keep the library clean and orderly. During the school year, shelves won't always be neat, but it's best to clear books off the table and make an effort to straighten your desk. You never know who might be using your library after hours. It could be a board meeting or a parent association group. They will notice and report it.

Dusting counter tops and shelves is not always part of the regular custodial routine. Tables do need cleaning, preferably daily. Although it's not part of your job description, you may need to decide whether to do some cleaning or allow the library to look shopworn.

In most places odors are not an issue, but carpets that have not been cleaned for years can hold smells. Mold is dangerous as well as smelly. If you spot it, report to your principal and express concern.

If food has been served in the library for a function during or after school, the aroma lingers on. Coffee is notorious for hanging in the air. Unfortunately, student bodies add to the smells. If students come to the library after they have had gym or recess, it can be a problem.

Food and, particularly coffee, is the prime cause of stains in carpeting. As part of your end-of-year routines you can request the carpeting be cleaned. It doesn't always happen.

If you should have the opportunity to purchase carpeting for your library, consider carpet tiles as the squares are more easily replaced when necessary. Beyond looking at colors and other decorative aspects of flooring, explore which options provide the best sound control and resist mold.

Plants, in addition to making the library look welcoming, minimize odors. Also consider diffusers and essential oils. Avoid anything that is too powerful. You don't want the library to smell like a cleaned public restroom.

Review your space on a regular basis. You can stop seeing things if you don't make a point of focusing on them. When you walk in on a Monday, what message is the library sending? No one will tell you if it's getting tired and dusty looking, but they will react. Make sure your library continues to be welcoming.

THE NAME GAME

Names are important. If you can address someone by name, you show you recognize them as a person. Being able to pronounce names properly shows you care. But as a school librarian you have a huge challenge. An elementary teacher only has to learn the names of the twenty-five to thirty students in their class. A high school teacher may need to learn the names of 125 to 175 students. But you encounter many, many more students in the library.

You see the whole school and have only a short time with each group on an irregular basis. In a high school you may easily have upwards of one thousand students. It is almost impossible to learn all the names. However, the more names you know, the more effective you will be.

Elementary librarians may have a roster or can get one for the classes they see. Have students pronounce their names and state what they wish to be called. Does Deborah want you to use her whole name, or Debbie or Deb? Repeat their name and note pronunciation and preferred nicknames on the roster. Many elementary librarians use a seating chart similar to what is used in classrooms. Once you have mastered their names, you can let students sit wherever they wish.

Middle and high school librarians develop a variety of strategies. You can ask any of the regulars for their names. Let them know you are working at learning names, and it probably will take a while before you remember all of them. Try to learn a set number of names each week.

If the teacher is present during orientation, have the kids complete a paste-on name tag. This will help you get started. Don't try it when students are without their teacher as they are apt to get creative with their names.

Because you can't always get a mini research project started early enough for orientations, have students explore something they love to do or are most interested in. Give them only a short time. As part of the project have them include some pictures. This will also give you the opportunity to show them some online resources they can use.

One requirement of this assignment it that a student must put their name on it. Their interests can suggest a mnemonic to remind you who they are. And this will be a jumping-off point for building relationships, which will further cement their names in your head.

To be honest, I always struggled to remember student names. I have problems remembering names in general. But I shared my difficulty with the kids, and they knew I kept working at it. By contrast, my late co-author Ruth Toor, who was an elementary librarian with a flexible schedule much like a middle or high school librarian, managed to learn the names of all 600 students in her school. Being honest when you aren't successful helps build trust and relationships.

Other ways to remember names are available online. The ones directed towards teachers have good ideas but often presume you are dealing with fewer people than you will face. Todd Finley has some basic suggestions that are worth checking out.[3] They are meant for classroom teachers, but some will work with a bit of adaptation. Creating name tents helps at the elementary level, but it is not practical with upper grades.

If you school is small, you stand a good chance of getting to know everyone's names in a month or so, but it is virtually an impossible task at larger schools. You will get to know your regulars and that will help. As someone who has always had trouble remembering names, I have learned to keep asking. I let kids know it's a challenge for me, and I need their help. The fact that you are obviously working at it shows you care, and students will react positively.

LEARNING AND BEHAVIORAL THEORISTS

Underneath all teaching is a philosophy you hold about learning, which is also known as epistemology. For centuries, philosophers have been looking at how we learn, and their impact is till reflected today. The twentieth century saw more learning and behavioral theorists, and their ideas and impact are reflected, in various degrees, in education today. Although theories go in and out of favor, depending on politics and other pressures, you should be familiar with the theorists' names and their approaches to education.

If you are a classroom teacher, you have studied many of them, but it helps to review them in light of learning in the library. As you read about each reflect on which ones are most aligned with your views about your role in student learning. Go back to the philosophy you wrote and make additions, drawing on the thinking of those theorists who make the most sense to you.

Richard Millwood created a graphic featuring twenty theorists that shows their interconnected areas of learning and behavior.[4] You probably won't be interested in all of them, but you can see which ones are similar and in what ways. Terry Heick included it in his article "Thirty-Two Learning Theories Every Teacher Should Know."[5] Heick discusses the various theories, from instructivism, scientific pedagogy, and constructivism, to scaffolding, discovery learning, problem-based learning, and blended or combination learning. His definitions are brief, and you can quickly see which you want to explore further, and his explanations will be helpful in understanding the theories of the people listed below.

This is my list of theorists whose work has relevance for the school library classroom:

John Dewey (1859–1952). Known as the father of progressive education, Dewey believed in learning through doing. He saw the old educational system as based on the belief that pure being is changeless. By contrast, Dewey rejected rote learning because he considered learning to be about change and that nothing is static. He felt learning needed to be meaningful and related to students' interests and their lives. In Dewey's view, the school should be a microcosm of democracy.

Maria Montessori (1870–1952). A doctor and educator, Montessori developed an interest in the learning of children with disabilities and determined that their delinquent behavior was the result of their not getting the education they needed in the way they needed it. When working with children in a town where children went largely unsupervised, she discovered they were capable of teaching themselves when given tasks that followed their natural development. Her theory is known as cosmic education. The key principles are:

- independence
- observation
- following the child
- correcting the child
- prepared environment
- absorbent mind

Montessori schools worldwide work from these principles.

Lev Vygotsky (1896–1934). As Dewey's ideas were connected to his views on democracy, Vygotsky, a Soviet psychologist, tied his to Marxism. He believed learners needed to interact with adults and older children. He introduced the concepts of the zone of proximal development (ZPD) and scaffolding. ZPD refers to the place between what a child already knows and what they can learn from an adult. It is in the overlap that learning occurs. (ZPD is similar to the third space in guided inquiry as presented by Leslie Maniotes.[6]) Scaffolding refers to giving students support to help them complete a learning task. As they become more proficient less scaffolding is given until none is needed.

Jean Piaget (1896–1980). Piaget's theory of cognitive development detailed the stages all children pass through. They may do so at somewhat different speeds, but they proceed from one stage to the next without skipping any. He identified the following four stages of cognitive development:

- sensorimotor (birth to age 2)
- pre-operational (ages 2–7)
- concrete operational (7–11)
- formal operational (11 and up)

In the sensorimotor stage, the infant learns that an object that is hidden is still there (peek-a-boo) and learns through sucking and touching. At the pre-operational stage, children use words and pictures to represent objects. In the concrete operational stage, children think logically and can understand that a tall, thin glass is holding less water than a shorter, wide one. When they reach the formal operational stage, children can reason abstractly and use logic to deduce answers to problems.

Benjamin Bloom (1913–1999). All educators must be familiar with his three taxonomies—cognitive, affective, and psychomotor. Bloom is known for mastery learning, which proposes that all students can master learning if given the time and tools. He believed in objectives. Searching online for "Bloom verbs" yields numerous words to use in creating objectives for each level of his taxonomies. The revision of his cognitive taxonomy has at its base remember, which is simple recall, and moves upward through understand, apply, analyze evaluate, and create, as the learner progresses to higher-order thinking skills. Iowa State University's Center for Excellence in Learning and Teaching has an excellent explanation of the levels, the words that indicate them, and the knowledge dimensions for each.[7]

Jerome Bruner (1915–2016). A constructivist, Bruner believed students learn by constructing new knowledge based on what they know and the opportunities they have to interact with new information. He proposed that we learn first through enactive learning, which is action-based; then iconic learning, which is image-based; and finally, symbolic learning, which is language-based. He thought students in an elementary classroom should acquire new knowledge the way a scientist in the field does. To do that he believed scaffolding should be used to help learners progress. He theorized that infants have the intellectual capabilities of adults, are good at problem-solving, and, with the development of language, become able to understand the world around them.

David A. Kolb (1939–). Kolb's leaning theory is composed of a four-stage experiential cycle:

- concrete experience
- reflective observation of the new experience
- abstract conceptualization
- active experimentation

The concrete experience is triggered by a new experience or a new view of something already known. In the next stage, there is reflection on any inconsistencies between the experience and the understanding. Abstract conceptualization is what was learned through the experience. And in the final stage, active experimentation, the learner applies the new ideas. He also proposed four learning styles:

- diverging—information gatherers, emotional perceivers, and observers
- assimilating—learners who focus on ideas and logic
- converging—those learners who apply practical solutions
- accommodating—hands-on learners who trusts their "guts"

The experiential cycle and the learning styles are formed into a two-column, two-row matrix.

Neil Fleming (1939–). Fleming identified four channels of learning or modalities that are indicated by the acronym *VARK*—visual, aural/auditory, read/write, and kinesthetic. Visual learners prefer charts, maps, infographics, diagrams, and other visual representations. Aural/auditory learners favor podcasts, lectures, webinars, chats, and other listening resources. Read/write learners do best with books, e-books, and other printed materials because words are central to them. Kinesthetic learners like demonstrations and simulations, hands-on work, case studies, and such. (Compare VARK with Gardner's multiple intelligences and Kolb's four learning styles.)

Howard Gardner (1943–). Known for his theory of multiple intelligences, Gardner postulated originally that there were seven types of intelligence: verbal/linguistic, mathematical/logical, musical intelligence, visual/spatial, bodily/kinesthetic, interpersonal, and intrapersonal. He later added natural intelligence (the ability to recognize and categorize plants and animals), and existential intelligence (the ability to explore the deep questions such as the meaning of life) and further expanded the list to humor, cooking, and sex. However, most educators stick to the first seven. What Gardner's theories showed is that because schools assess students only on verbal/linguistic and mathematical/logical intelligences, they fail to capture the full picture of students' intelligence. Indeed, being gifted either verbally or mathematically is no guarantee of success or achievement. Those with high interpersonal abilities fare much better.

These behavior and learning theorists' views are written in academic terminology that can be hard to wade through. Look for sources that summarize their work and make it easier to access. There is overlap in views among them.

It may be helpful to refer to Richard Millbrook's visual and Terry Heick's overviews of learning theories. You may find other theorists whose work aligns with your philosophy. Knowing their thinking as well as your beliefs and values will help as you interact with students and construct your lessons.

🔲 KEY IDEAS

- What your library looks like sends the first message as to whether it's a safe, welcoming space.
- Furniture needs to be age appropriate and varied.
- Bookcases should not block sight lines. Get a security mirror if they do.
- Signs should be colorful, help users find their way with a minimum of confusion, and use words that have meaning for students.
- Bulletin boards and displays should excite interest and be changed frequently.
- Display student work as much as possible and feature their accomplishments.
- Plants add to the look and feel of the library.
- Become familiar with your automated system so you can input new students and teachers and check books in and out.
- Meet with the principal to fix the last date for check out.
- Orientations set the tone for how students see you and the library.
- Orientations are generally conducted each year at the elementary grades.
- Middle and high school orientations are usually given only to the incoming class usually, with the ELA teacher.
- Think through the purpose of your orientations. What do you want students to take away? Use questions to determine what students already know about libraries, including their likes and dislikes.
- The orientation should be fun as well as informative.
- Be aware of your body language and tone of voice as you greet students with a smile.
- Connecting the orientation to a mini research project makes it more long-lasting.
- To foster a welcoming environment, emphasize expectations rather than rules.
- Expectations should be stated positively.
- Discuss expectations with students and have them suggest some of their own.
- Food and drink are now permitted in many libraries.
- The decision whether to permit it should be based on your philosophy, mission, and vision, with input from custodians, administrators, and teachers.
- Carpet odors, dust, and students' body odor can make for unpleasant scents. Use plants, diffusers, essential oils or air fresheners to keep the library smelling nice.

- Look at your library with fresh eyes every Monday to be sure it is continuing to send a welcoming message.
- It makes a difference if you can call students by their names.
- School librarians come in contact with far more students than classroom teachers, which makes it challenging and possibly impossible to learn all their names.
- Elementary librarians need rosters for all the classes they see, with notes on pronunciations and preferred nicknames.
- Middle and high school librarians should ask kids their names when they come in and apologize in advance for not being able to remember everyone.
- Try a research project for orientation that has middle and high school students doing something that will help you remember their names.
- Name tents and name tags are possible aids. You'll find more suggestions online.
- Explore the ideas of various learning and behavioral theorists to determine which theories are closely aligned with your thinking and beliefs.
- Review the work of the theorists and discover what most resonates with your beliefs; review your philosophy to see if you need to add to it.

NOTES

1. "Quotable Quotes: C. H. Spurgeon," Goodreads, https://www.goodreads.com/quotes/744825-begin-as-you-mean-to-go-on-and-go-on.
2. Terry Heick, "Twelve Questions to Ask Your Students on the First Day of School," *TeachThought*, August 9, 2019, https://www.teachthought.com/pedagogy/12-questions-ask-students-first-day-school/?fbclid=IwAR1vCGjW_y5ZJHqiH3_E5k3cISlNmRiXHXUCnkjbpE_gHcNurUP8U1WE4Xo.
3. Todd Finley, "How to Remember Students' Names," *Edutopia* (blog), August 22, 2017, https://www.edutopia.org/blog/what-did-you-call-me-how-remember-students-names.
4. R. Millwood, "Learning Theory," *TeachThought*, https://www.teachthought.com/wp-content/uploads/2018/12/learning-theory-overview.png.
5. Terry Heick, "Thirty-Two Learning Theories Every Teacher Should Know," *TeachThought*, ,July 27, 2019, https://www.teachthought.com/learning/a-visual-summary-the-most-important-learning-theories/.
6. L. Maniotes, "Third Space in Guided Inquiry," 2005, https://sjelib.weebly.com/uploads/2/8/1/3/28130057/2-6_thirdspaceinguidedinquirydiagram.pdf.
7. "Revised Bloom's Taxonomy," Iowa State University: Center for Excellence in Learning and Teaching, www.celt.iastate.edu/teaching/effective-teaching-practices/revised-blooms-taxonomy/.

3
A Library Lesson

Lesson planning is central to teaching. At the elementary level, you will probably be required to turn in your lesson plans. If so, you will be given a format to follow. At upper grades this isn't always expected of the librarian, but until you are fully confident and comfortable in your role as teacher, you should keep doing them. Even experienced school librarians gain much from preparing lesson plans. In addition to keeping you focused, they become a record of what you have done, what worked, and what didn't.

If you aren't given a form to follow, search online for lesson templates. There are many to choose from. Select one that fits your style. It should have a place for most of the following elements:

- curricular connections—yours and the teachers
- standards addressed—AASL's *National School Library Standards*, state standards, ISTE standards
- assessments—formative and summative
- essential questions (and, preferably, enduring understandings)
- goals/objectives
- activities/tasks
- student outcomes

PLANNING A LESSON

Preparing a library lesson is both similar and different from a classroom lesson. Obviously, it should be connected to your curriculum. At the middle and high school levels it will also be part of the classroom teacher's curriculum.

As a classroom teacher would, you begin by identifying why you are teaching the lesson. An elementary storytime may focus on empathy. A middle school lesson might be on nutrition. A high school might focus on fake news. Using those three examples, you should be able to identify your purpose.

Begin at the end. Now that you know your purpose, what takeaways do you want students to get from the lesson? The answer gives you the *enduring understanding* each lesson should have. An enduring understanding for the empathy lesson might be, "Caring about other people's feelings makes me feel good about myself." For nutrition, "Nutrition labels give me valuable information for making good choices." For fake news, "I am responsible for determining the accuracy of the information I use."

You may have more than one enduring understanding in mind. Students are likely to take away others. A good lesson stays with students long after it is completed, and its takeaway can change over time as they reflect on it in later years. And yes, even in later years, some units can have a strong impact on students' thinking.

Next, determine what *essential questions* drive the lesson. For example, "How can I be a more caring person?" "What can be done to help people have a healthy lifestyle?" "How does fake news spread?" There are many other questions and students can and should come up with on their own during the course of the lesson. Note that answers to essential questions cannot be found by doing a Google search. Like enduring understandings, students' answers to essential questions can change over the years.

Recognize that children learn differently and structure your lessons to allow for this. On the one hand, differentiated learning is more challenging for librarians because they do not know these students as well as the teacher does. On the other hand, the library is the perfect environment for such differentiation.

Get as much information from the teacher as you can about students who will benefit from differentiated learning However, if you incorporate a variety of learning activities in the lesson, you will be able to address multiple needs. For an explanation of differentiated learning and how to implement it in the content, process, products, and learning environment, see *Reading Rockets,* "What Is Differentiated Instruction?" (https://www.readingrockets.org/article/what-differentiated-instruction).

Formative evaluations are ongoing throughout a lesson and let you monitor students' understanding of the content. Teachers have always monitored faces to see if students were engaged or looked confused or bored. Another quick check is to ask students to put a thumb up if they understand, put their thumb to the side if they are somewhat confused, and turn it down if they have no clue about what they are supposed to do or learn. Your questions throughout the lesson are also formative in nature and you can use pair/share when appropriate.

You also need a summative assessment. A test is the classic summative evaluation, but there are other ways to determine what students have learned. It doesn't matter what you taught. It's what they learned that counts. Exit tickets that have students responding to the lesson are a simple way to gather that information. (More on assessment will be discussed in chapter 9.)

Unlike a classroom teacher, you have many different classes in a day, so you need to pause and consider the grade and subject you are teaching as you design the lesson and prepare its content. Use what you have learned and will be learning to match your lesson to the attention spans and interests of the students. At all ages, students will tune out and become disruptive when there is a disconnect between what you are teaching and where they are.

I once observed an elementary librarian who read Hans Christian Andersen's "The Emperor's New Clothes" to a first-grade class. By the end of the lesson, students were falling to the side, subtly and not so subtly kicking one another, and were unable and uninterested in answering any questions at the conclusion.

The librarian had made a number of mistakes. They grabbed a book without thinking about it. . They didn't do a lesson plan. The story focuses on being vain and complicit, which are not themes that resonate with first graders. The vocabulary in the version they chose was too difficult for them; they were unfamiliar with words like *courtier, chamberlain,* and *scoundrel*, and they never explained them. They were bored and showed it.

I once made a mistake by reading Marcia Brown's *Stone Soup* to a first grade class. It had worked well with second graders, but that one year made all the difference. The story is short, so they paid attention, but my mistake showed quickly when I asked them about the trick used to make the soup. They believed that the hungry soldiers who had started the soup from stones and used that ploy to get the villagers to contribute food to the pot had literally made soup from stones. It completely went over their heads.

STANDARDS

Lesson plans need to address the standards that students are expected to attain. Classroom teachers must identify the state curricular standard and ensure the lesson addresses it. For several years this meant the Common Core State Standards (CCSS), but most states have gone to their own standards, which are similar but not quite the same as CCSS. Your state's Department of Education should have them online.

Although you should let the classroom teacher know what you are doing, that doesn't always happen at the elementary level. Nevertheless, you need to know which of your state standards apply to the lesson. Include that information at the beginning of your lesson plans to show the contribution you are making to the curriculum.

As a school librarian, you need to know the standards for all the grade levels in your school. At the elementary level you will regularly refer to the same ones because you meet classes on fixed schedule. Middle and high school librarians must be familiar with ELA standards and check the others as different subject area teachers plan projects in the library.

You also should address the American Association of School Librarian's (AASL) *National School Library Standards for Learners, School Librarians, and School Libraries* (2018).[1] The Common Beliefs are reflected in your philosophy, and the four Domains and six Shared Foundations form the Competencies you want students to achieve. As the title suggests, there are three sets of standards: one for learners, one for school librarians, and one for school libraries. In preparing your plans use the given frameworks to help you incorporate all three standards.[2]

The International Society for Technology in Education (ISTE) also has standards that apply to school librarians.[3] Download them and familiarize yourself with these as well. Unlike AASL, ISTE covers several areas within the school system including computer teachers and the technology department. Your principal is apt to like the *ISTE Standards,* so demonstrating how these are incorporated into you lessons shows your value to the educational program.

OPENING

Preparation is vital, particularly when you are new. After several years you will have enough experience to develop your lessons and units much more quickly, and in a pinch, you will be able to create one on the fly. But your time with the class isn't just the core of the lesson. Every lesson has a beginning, a middle, and an end. Planned transitions ensure students move seamlessly from one part to the next with little or no disruption.

The strategies for managing each part is different. If each part is not handled appropriately, the lesson will not be successful. If a football team played its end game the way it plays the middle part, it would lose. The same is true for you.

To recognize each of the three major sections of a lesson, we will look at each part individually; first, the openings for the different grade levels; then the middle, which is the content of the lesson; and finally, the ending, when you bring it to a close. This helps you focus on each part individually and shows you the similarities and differences as you go up the grades.

In the opening, the game plan is to get students into the library in an orderly fashion and be prepared and focused on what is to come. Because of the number of classes you see in a day, establishing a routine takes a bit of time, but if it isn't in place you will be playing catch-up throughout the lesson. Classroom teachers can post their routines, but because their students are already in the room, this is easy. Your students come in for a single period and then leave. You may not even have a spot where they could review your list of routines and expectations (and in any case, the very youngest students can't read them).

Primary and Elementary Grades

Students are dropped off at the door to your library. Some teachers may barely say hello to you before heading for their breaks. Prevent a scramble as students barrel into the wide-open space that your library represents to them by greeting them at the door with a welcoming smile.

Until you have established your opening routine, have students remain in a line outside the library as you guide them inside and into their seats. Keep your roster handy and have numbers placed on each table. As students enter hand them name cards that include their table number. This both helps you remember their name and directs them to where they should sit for the opening. Continue this practice at least for the first two months until you know their names. You may want to keep it up throughout the year because it helps to begin the class with them knowing exactly where to sit.

As students enter have them drop off the books they are returning, either in a book drop or on a cart before they take their seats. Even after they know how to enter the library, meet the class outside but talk briefly to one or two students as they enter. You might comment on something they are wearing or note that you have a book they might like. This sends and reinforces your message that the library is a safe welcoming place.

The entry needs to proceed as expeditiously as possible. Move into the library as more of the class enters so you can keep an eye on the students who are supposed to be going to their assigned tables. Remember that the attention span for primary students is extremely short. If they have too much time they will be wiggling and bothering each other.

For a list of procedures and routines, some of which you might want to add to your expectations, review "Library Procedures: A Guide to Sanity" at the *Elementary Librarian* website.[4] Although it is designed for classroom teachers, you can get some good ideas from Hannah Hudson's "Twelve Must-Teach Classroom Procedures and Routines."[5]

The simplest technique to move the class to the area where you will be reading a story is an easy call and response. Clap your hands together in a rhythmic pattern and have students repeat it. The first few times you will have to remind them to do it and then wait for your directions. If you always go to the storytime area, they can move after everyone is focused on you.

Third and fourth graders are not quite as itchy, but they have been in school long enough to know when they aren't being observed. They too are likely to fool around. It takes longer to get a class back on track once you have lost them than to ensure that this opening piece is orderly and efficient.

The first step is usually book return. At first, call tables up to put their returned books on a cart. Later on, they can place their books there as they enter. It's best to save book selection and checkout for the end because students are likely to spend time looking at their choices and not following any directions you are giving.

Moving from the opening to the middle part of the lesson is the first transition. It's during transitions that kids most often become disengaged. A bell is a frequently used too to let students know it's time for a change.

You then need something to move them into the core of the lesson. My favorite simple technique is to use "entrance tickets." They signal students that the lesson itself is about to begin and focuses their thinking on the topic. If you were doing a lesson on kindness and empathy, some questions might be, "Was anyone kind to you today? "Were you kind to anyone?" "How did that make you feel?

Middle School

Classes most commonly arrive with their teacher, who remains but may be an active participant, a mostly silent presence, or off somewhere in the library. Book return is not part of the routine because students can return and check out books as needed. Although the frequency of when you see classes is up to the teacher—and your ability to create collaborations—you still need a routine.

You will quickly be able to see different teachers' management styles. Some classes enter quietly and wait to be directed to where you want them to sit. Others seem to explode into the library. Once you are familiar with the various teachers you will be more prepared for the differences.

These students are older, but they still should be welcomed with a smile. That's always the first rule. If their entrance is not orderly, quickly demonstrate your ability to manage. Keep it positive. You can say, "I am glad to see you are all so enthusiastic. Let's see what I can do to help you today." If you have your expectations posted, point to the list as a brief reminder.

If you don't plan a way for students to enter the library, expect some pushing and shoving. If the teacher is alert it may not happen, but this is your space and you are responsible for it. Think of middle school as having a high school–style schedule with similar types of learning projects but done with elementary kids. These students are older than elementary students, but still "itchy," because of sudden growth spurts and the start of puberty.

Direct students to the area in which they are to sit. If you have planned the class with the teacher, they can tell their students where to go. Even if the lesson will require them to be at computers, have them start out at tables. Otherwise, they will go online and completely tune you out.

For teachers who have brought their classes but don't want your help, indicate where students should sit. Ask the teacher if the class will need anything. Usually, you will be told that nothing is necessary, but, as much as possible, observe how students are doing once the class has started. Invariably they do need help.

When you are working collaboratively or cooperatively with teachers, use entrance tickets or some other quick opening to get the students thinking before moving on to the project itself. You can have the paper tickets or use a SMART Board or a program like Google Slides. For the lesson on nutrition, ask, "What is your most favorite and least favorite food?" "Can you name one unhealthy food?" "What makes it unhealthy?"

Have them work with another student. This gives them an opportunity to talk as well as to start thinking about the topic. Give them five minutes or less to complete the task, and then ask for their responses. This serves several purposes. You have not only settled the class, but you have also started students thinking about the topic. From their responses you will learn what aspects of the subject interest them, which will move them naturally into an inquiry-based project.

High School

Your routine at the high school level is similar to middle school. Ideally, you should work with almost all subject areas, but in practice most of your classes will come from English or history. Invariably they will be doing research. In the best-case scenario, as in middle school, you and the teacher will have planned out the enduring understandings and essential questions. Students may already have their topics.

Student behavior at this level is both better and worse. You don't get the pushing and shoving behavior (although you might still see some from ninth graders). A lot depends on how well the teacher manages the class. If teachers allow a lot of freewheeling in their classes, it will be the same in the library unless you are prepared to step in.

Again, you need an opening activity to settle the class and have them mentally prepared for the lesson. For the high school unit on fake news, entrance tickets can ask, "Where do you get your news?" "How do you decide if it's true?" Having students work in pairs sets the tone for collaborative work from the beginning. Sharing answers also can help students home in on the specific topic they would like to explore if it wasn't preassigned.

MIDDLE SECTION

This is the heart of the lesson, where content is delivered, and students become engaged with their learning. In designing this section, determine which of several current approaches will work best with a particular project. These are some to consider:

- *Inquiry-based learning.* Students use what they know to develop questions they wish to explore further. Previous knowledge, from what was learned in class or a preliminary search, is needed so they have the background to formulate the questions. The Key Commitment for the Shared Foundation of Inquire is "build new knowledge by inquiring, thinking critically, identifying a problem, and developing a strategy for solving that problem."[6] A *Knowledge Quest* blog post, "The Five E's of Inquiry-Based Learning," does an excellent job of explaining the approach.[7]
- *Project-based learning.* Students are given, or preferably self-select, a real-world problem and then engage in various activities to develop a solution. Students share as they are learning and collaborate with each other. The Key Commitment for the Shared Foundation of Collaborate is "work effectively with others to broaden perspectives and work toward common goals."[8]
- *Problem-based learning.* Similar to project-based learning, students are challenged to solve a real-world problem which may or may not be assigned. The main distinction is whether it's a project or the focus is on a specific problem. The Key Commitment for the Shared Foundation of Curate is "make meaning for oneself and others by collecting, organizing, and sharing resources of personal relevance."[9]
- *Design-based learning.* Working in groups, student design a product. For each step of the process they learn something new that they put into effect, learning from failure and success. The Key Commitment for the Shared Foundation of Explore is "discover and innovate in a growth mindset developed through experience and reflection."[10]

Whatever the approach, move among student groups as they work to monitor their progress. Avoid telling them what to do; instead, ask guiding questions that help them solve their problems by themselves.

All four of these approaches are student-centered, giving them "voice and choice" in their learning. They keep students engaged, and engaged students rarely act out. However, you must handle the transition from the opening to the learning experience smoothly so that you don't lose students.

In designing your lessons at all grade levels, recognize that students learn differently. That is the reasoning behind differentiated instruction. The concept fits in well with school library projects. Your challenge is to discover how to tailor the differentiation based on student needs. Practice will help you get there. This is explained in Cathy Weselby's "What Is Differentiated Instruction? Examples of How to Differentiate in the Classroom."[11]

Primary and Elementary Grades

The lesson itself is divided into several parts, each of which will have a transition. The most common opening is to start with a story. School librarians need to be adept at holding up a book so children can always see the pictures and moving the book from one hand to the next while reading the text Ask questions about what is happening and have students predict what will happen next based on the illustrations. At the conclusion, talk about the story, ensuring they got the message and tying it back to the entrance ticket.

Kindergarten to Grade 2

Kindergartners can't sit still for more than one story in a row. You will need an activity that gets them up and moving. Choose a transition technique. Use the same hand-clapping signal you used at the beginning of the lesson. Ring a bell to get kids' attention and have them stop whatever they were doing. Then you can say, "When I ring the bell again, everyone stand up." Either connect a very brief activity to the story or do something as simple as having them stretch high and then touch their nose. This gets the wiggles out. You can find many more suggestions online.

Ring the bell again and direct them to their next activity. It could be another short story. Be sure to introduce it with enough context and background. As with the example of *The Emperor's New Clothes*, be mindful of the length, language, and subject of the story. For PK to grade 4, picture books that focus on empathy as a theme may be appropriate for some grades but not for others. Choose wisely.

After each story, use your essential questions as a guide when leading students in a brief discussion of the core issues. Ask them to make observations about the plot or illustrations. Kindergartners and first graders are masters of the non sequitur. If you may hear something like "My aunt just had a baby," smile in response and say, "We can have some time for sharing when we line up at the end. Right now we are talking about the story."

When you have finished reading, have students address how the stories are connected. For the inquiry-based component, students can either draw (drawing is equivalent to writing at this level) a new ending, suggest a better choice, or show how a character from one of the stories would act upon meeting a character from another story.

You could also present a lesson. Book care is often a topic. Although part of the elementary library curriculums, it can be boring. A story can make it more interesting. You can combine the lesson with one on selecting books.

Display a well-rounded assortment of books on tables and countertop bookcases from which students can choose. Have them pick up any book. Ask them how you turned the pages when you were reading the story. Let them work in pairs with one watching the other doing, then switching as they turn some pages in the books they are holding. It's not necessary to go through an entire book.

Ring the bell again and announce that they will have time to choose books they want to read, but first have them tell you how they will take care of their book so that it will be ready for the next person to borrow it. To avoid chaos, have one table at a time choose books from those out on display while students at the other tables can continue to practice handling a book.

An excellent alternative to having students wait while others check out is to set up learning centers where they are engaged and learning and keep them from being bored and getting into mischief. Jessica Lodge has posted a PDF of a presentation that encapsulates the benefits for you and the students and gives directions on getting started and has helpful illustrations.[12]

If you have a clerk (which is very rare these days) or volunteers, students can check out their selections immediately, learning how to do so as they go through the process. Otherwise check out students one table at a time. To make it fair—and interesting—put the table numbers in a pretty box so you or different kids can draw the numbers.

Some librarians don't permit students to check out another book unless they have returned one. I don't like to put any barriers to student reading. There are many reasons for a student to return a book late, including leaving it in the home of one parent and not having a chance to pick it up. If you keep them from taking a book out, the message you send is that acting responsibly is more important than reading.

I prefer to put a form into a student's newly checked-out book that states that they still have another book that hasn't been returned. If you charge fines, you will have to sequence check in and book selection as the first part of the lesson. Many libraries are dispensing with fines, rightfully seeing them as a barrier to reading.

Elementary lessons vary from thirty to forty-five minutes long depending on the school. For K–2, thirty minutes will feel long enough, particularly at the start of the school year, but with third and fourth graders, fitting a lesson, a story, and book selection into a half-hour can seem hurried. You can do stories one week and a lesson another, but at the beginning include both.

Grades 3–5

Greeting students at the door and smiling is always the best way to set the tone for the lesson. If this isn't your first year in the school, students will know the entrance routine you expect. When you are new, you will have to show them.

Book return is first, freeing them for the other activities. You can eventually have a rotating pair of students load the books onto a cart. They can even put them in shelf order so that they are easier to shelve once they are checked in (which will be another one of your jobs if you don't have an aide or volunteers).

Have entrance tickets on the table for students to begin discussing with another student or post the questions on a SMART Board or a slide share program. For a lesson on community, you can ask them "What's the best thing about living in our town?" or "What would you like to see here that we don't have?"

Students in grades 3–5 have a longer attention span than the littles, but it's still limited. Balance your lessons between stories and the beginning to teach them about research. Listening to a story builds literacy and encourages lifelong reading but use it as a springboard to other things. For example, for a lesson about community, you might read Chris Van Dusen's *If I Built a House* and challenge students to work in pairs to build something special of their own that could be a great addition to the community. It could be a playground, a theme restaurant, or a rocket-powered tour of the town. (Note that the Van Dusen book is a picture book, so you'll need to explain to fourth and fifth graders that you are using it for an example, or they are likely to be offended.)

A related follow-up could give students some time at your makerspace to work on their ideas. Have some helpful books on display. Take pictures of their creations. If there is time, show them how to locate books related to their topics using the OPAC or save that for the next lesson. Or turn this into more of a research project by having them show their creations and explain how they created them by sharing with other students or posting on your website. Give them a simple format to use for citing their sources. It's best to teach ethical use of information early.

Middle School

Middle schoolers will work similarly to students in grades 3–5. As noted, their attention span is somewhat better, but they are of an age when some are beginning puberty and hormones come into play. Because you likely have a flexible schedule you might have a few days in a row to complete the project.

If they are working on nutrition, move smoothly from the responses they gave for the opening questions. Add a few more questions such as "What are some healthy foods you like?" Coordinate these with a list you created or developed with the teacher on different aspects of nutrition. It is best if this is done before the class comes to the library along with giving students the chance to pick their topic. (In chapter 4 we will discuss collaboration in detail.)

Hand out a checklist of what students need to complete. This gives them a guide for the steps they are to follow in the research process. One of the first items should be a list of questions they want to explore. Have students work in groups on a topic. Remind them to keep track of their sources and include sample citations for different types of resources.

Cover the tables with dry erase paper so they can create mind maps to get a sense of where they want to go. Encouraging them to get up and move while they're focusing works well with students of this age. Take photos of their work for them to refer to when they return. Create a LibGuide on sources students can use for the project.

High School

High school students are already accustomed to coming to the library for research. The challenge is that they think they know how to do it and are likely to tune out your instructions. Give them ten minutes to get started on what they think they are doing, then call them back to reflect on their process.

What were they searching for? Where did they go to find it? How successful were they? Although students are relatively good at searching, they are poor at research. Let them know this is where they will discover how to get where they want to go in the most efficient way. Share the process (e.g., guided inquiry) that you want them to follow so that they learn the steps.

For the lesson on fake news, you can use what Debra Gottsleben and Anne Piascik, two librarians at New Jersey's Morristown High School, (New Jersey) put together.[13] They created a health-based LibGuide on fake news that forms the basis of the lesson. They present a short and simple video (which they admit is a little cheesy), that kids will like. They conclude with a discussion of what students learned from the video.

Next, they count students off by sixes and put them into different numbered groups. The groups review the video that is part of the case study for their group number. Using Google Docs, they must do a presentation on why they think it is real or fake. Each person must contribute one reason that no one else in the group used. This exercise encourages insightful analysis.

CLOSING

Moving from the middle of the lesson to the closing is a major transition that can become chaotic if not planned. Keep an eye on the clock to ensure you have enough time to have a smooth conclusion.

Primary and Elementary Grades

Book checkout traditionally completes the lesson. If you don't save it for the end it will eat up too much time. Use your transition signal to move students to the table where they began. This rounds out the lesson by returning to the start of the circle.

Have one or two tables search for their books while the others look at books you have placed on tables for browsing. While the first tables begin checking out the next group begins. In grades four and five, groups of students may be able to select their books simultaneously. If you have a self-checkout system this can work well.

You want students to check out books that appeal to them, but in far too many schools they are constrained by being limited to books on their instructional level. When that applies to a classroom collection, it's not a problem. However, you need to do whatever you can to prevent that policy from affecting what students borrow from the library.

When students choose books below their reading levels, they develop reading fluency. When they choose books above their reading levels, they develop persistence. But mostly, they discover the love of reading.

Accelerated Reader (AR) and similar programs also can interfere with students selecting books they like. If students pass a test when they complete a book, they earn points. Sometimes they earn prizes. The competition inclines students to select books based on point value instead of choosing books they like with lower point values. It sounds at first as though this is a great incentive for students to read more challenging books. But the motivation—points and rewards—is extrinsic. Once the extrinsic rewards are removed when the students go on to a higher grade without AR, they may lose interest in reading.

Give your transition signal once checkout is complete and use exit tickets to bring the lesson to a close. Have students complete a "3, 2, 1" exercise: "Three things I learned, two things I found interesting, one question I still have." More exit ticket questions are readily available online. Collect them and use them as a summative assessment and to document the information for your administrators.

Regularly check if students can answer the essential questions. Be sure your essential questions really were essential. Lee Watanabe-Crockett suggests two steps to ensure they are.[14] First, move the question up the levels of Bloom's taxonomy so it goes further than knowledge, asking students to analyze and evaluate. Then keep specifics out of the question as much as possible. You want their thinking to go beyond thinking about the current assignment.

Although you should always have a closing activity, you don't always use the same one because kids get bored and turn it off. In an *Edutopia* blog post, Todd Finley offers twenty-two closure activities that give students the opportunity to reflect on a lesson and anchor it so they remember it.[15] Closing activities are a summative assessment for you and students of what was (and was not) learned. A closing activity also announces the lesson is over and prepares students for the final transition to exiting the library.

Finally, you need to have students line up in an orderly fashion by the door so their teacher can pick them up. Your bell or another transition method is the signal for them to get ready for this last part. Call them up table by table.

To help them keep hands to themselves, ask them to "hug their books." Smile. and let them know you enjoyed having them. If the teacher is not yet there you can ask them what their favorite part of library time was.

Middle and High Schools

At both these levels, book checkout occurs as needed throughout the lesson, and is only related to the project the class is working on rather than personal reading. You still need a closing activity because otherwise some students will shove their books into their backpacks and forget whatever they learned as soon as they walk out the door.

Try to leave five to ten minutes for a closing activity. Exit tickets will work because they are adaptable to the grade levels. You can also simply have students respond to statements that you might fit on an exit ticket such as, "The most important thing I learned was...," "This topic is important because...," or "I still need to find out..."

When a middle or high school teacher brings a class to the library and chooses not to have you do any teaching, you can ask the teacher if you can use a 3-2-1 exit ticket. This way you can help students with any follow-up. It is also a gentle way of letting the teacher know you are willing to work with them.

Anticipate the bell. In middle school, lining the kids up in advance is helpful. This is also useful at the high school level, but you can usually keep things orderly by standing at the door and letting students know you are watching them.

Even if you have a curriculum to follow, it's sometimes difficult to come up with another brilliant idea. It's sort of like dealing with that ongoing question of what's for dinner. Occasionally you draw a blank. Be prepared by bookmarking sites that are suitable for the grade levels you serve. You can find numerous ideas for library lessons on Pinterest and Teachers Pay Teachers, but remember that no matter how pretty they are, they won't all be good. Select from those that require students to think, question, and build new knowledge.

Give kids a two-minute warning that the period is about to end. Have them close out (and save if necessary) what they were doing on computers, and remind them to push their chairs in. Stand by the door as signal they are to begin lining up.

Teachers may have last minute instructions to give to students. Smile at those standing in line. You can chat briefly about anything, including how their work is going or that you like a tee-shirt they are wearing.

SPECIAL NEEDS STUDENTS

It is likely that some of your classes will include special needs students. To ensure that your lesson is aligned with their needs, you must first know who they are. These students will have an IEP (Individualized Education Program) or a 504 Plan on file. Because IEPs and 504 Plans are components of the Individuals with Disabilities Education Act (IDEA), you are legally responsible for complying with them.

We Are Teachers includes an excellent explanation of IEPs written by Elizabeth Mulvihill.[16] The advocacy organization Understood offers an overview of both IEPs and 504 Plans. Although intended for parents, the information is valuable for all.[17]

At the elementary level, ask teachers for this information as soon as possible. Put a symbol on your rosters so you remember who these students are. At the middle and high school levels, find out if any of the students teachers are bringing have an IEP and/or a 504 Plan and what you should be aware of and do for those students. You can also follow up by speaking with guidance counselors for information and suggestions. It is possible you may require some assistive technology for computers and other devices so that these students can make use of them.

If your school has special education students, their teachers may bring the class to the library. Usually these teachers are willing to work with you and are extremely helpful. I once worked regularly with a special education class. The results of this partnership are often extremely rewarding.

KEY IDEAS

- Writing lesson plans is valuable even if they are not required or you have experience teaching library classes.
- Use your school's lesson plan form or download a lesson plan template you like, making sure it includes all the necessary components.
- Identify your purpose for teaching the lesson.
- Know what enduring understandings you want students to take away.
- Essential questions drive the lesson and their answers won't be found by Googling.
- Include formative assessments throughout the lesson and plan for a summative assessment at the end.
- In planning your lesson, you consider the different attention spans and interests of students at several grade levels.
- Address the needs of all students through differentiated learning.
- Lessons must address your state's curricular standards.
- AASL's *National School Library Standards for Learners, School Librarians, and School Libraries* lists the Competencies students should attain as a result of a particular lesson.
- Address the standards for school librarians and school libraries as well as the one for learners.

- ISTE standards are important to know and also use in your lesson plans.
- Plan your lessons in three parts: an opening, a middle, and a conclusion or end.
- Always greet primary and elementary students at the door with a smile.
- For primary and elementary grade, use your roster to note student names, nicknames, and pronunciations as they enter.
- Begin by moving them quickly through the process of returning their books.
- Use a call and response (or a bell) to signal the end of the opening and direct students to the story area or where you will give a lesson.
- Entrance ticket questions get students thinking about the lesson to come.
- Middle school students are still apt to engage in pushing and shoving, so direct them quickly to a table to begin the lesson.
- Have students work in pairs to discuss their answers to entrance ticket questions and then share them. The whole activity shouldn't take much more than five minutes.
- Choose among guided inquiry, project-based learning, problem-based learning, and design-based learning in creating your lessons based on what your essential questions are.
- The school library program easily adapts to differentiated instruction.
- K–1 students can't sit for more than one story without needing some physical activity.
- These young students will often respond to your questions with unconnected information. Be prepared to focus them back on topic.
- Story discussions should address the essential question and guide students into thinking critically.
- Balance lessons for grades 3–5 between stories and lessons that are mini research projects.
- Teaching ethical use of information begins early. Show students simple ways to cite their sources.
- Move middle school students from the entrance question to the topics they will be researching, which ideally have been developed in conjunction with their teacher.
- Checklists of what needs to be completed help keep kids on track.
- Mind maps drawn on dry erase sheets help students focus on their research inquiry.
- LibGuides work well with both middle and high school students who are looking for sources to use in completing their projects.

- Book selection rounds out primary and elementary lessons.
- Requiring students to read books at their instructional level can work against building a love of reading.
- AR and similar programs offer extrinsic motivation to read. Once the rewards are gone, students will no longer choose to read if they never developed a love of reading.
- Having learning centers for use during checkout engages students during a time where they might get itchy.
- Use simple exit tickets such as "3-2-1" to bring the lesson to a close.
- Smile at primary and elementary students as they line up at the door to leave and let them know you enjoyed your time with them.
- Try to have a closing activity for middle and high school students even if the teacher didn't have you work with the class.
- Give middle and high school students a two-minute warning so they can complete what they are doing and push their chairs in.
- Ensure that middle and high school students exit in an orderly fashion by standing by the door to let them know you are watching them.
- Determine if any of your students have an IEP and/or a 504 Plan and what it entails.
- Working with special education students can be very rewarding for both you and the students.

NOTES

1. American Association of School Librarians, *National School Library Standards for Learners, School Librarians, and School Libraries* (Chicago: American Library Association, 2018).
2. AASL, *National School Library Standards*, 67–119.
3. International Society for Technology in Education, *ISTE Standards,* https://www.iste.org/standards.
4. "Library Procedures: A Guide to Sanity," *Elementary Librarian,* https://elementarylibrarian.com/library-procedures-guide-sanity/.
5. Hannah Hudson, "Twelve Must-Teach Classroom Procedures and Routines," *We Are Teachers,* 2019, https://www.weareteachers.com/classroom-procedures-save-sanity/.
6. AASL, *National School Library Standards*, 68–69.
7. S. Northern, "The Five E's of Inquiry-Based Learning," *Knowledge Quest* (blog), August 30, 2019, https://knowledgequest.aasl.org/the-5-es-of-inquiry-based-learning/.
8. AASL, *National School Library Standards*, 84–85.
9. AASL, *National School Library Standards*, 94–95.

10. AASL, *National School Library Standards,* 104–05.

11. C. Weselby, "What Is Differentiated Instruction? Examples of How to Differentiate in the Classroom," *Resilient Educator* (blog), March 2, 2020.

12. Jessica Lodge, "Library Centers in the Elementary School Classroom," *Mrs. Lodge's Library* (blog), 2015, www.mrs-lodges-library.com/media/MSLA_Library_Centers.pdf.

13. Debra Gottsleben and Anne Piascik, "Health: Detecting Fake News," Morristown (New Jersey) High School, http://mhs.msd.libguides.com/health/fakenews.

14. L. Watanabe-Crockett, "Two Simple Things That Will Make Essential Questions Better Every Time," *Wabisabi Learning*, 2019, https://wabisabistore.com/blogs/essential-questions/2-things-make-essential-questions-better.

15. T. Finley, "Twenty-Two Powerful Closure Activities," *Edutopia,* December 15, 2015, https://www.edutopia.org/blog/22-powerful-closure-activities-todd-finley.

16. E. Mulvihill, "What Exactly is an IEP?" *We Are Teachers*, February 28, 2018, https://www.weareteachers.com/what-is-an-iep/.

17. "What is an IEP?" *Understood,* https://www.understood.org/en/school-learning/special-services/ieps/what-is-an-iep.

4

Cooperation and Collaboration—and Co-Teaching

Knowing how to design a lesson plan and handle transitions is only the first part of presenting an effective school library activity. Students develop deeper understandings when their library lessons are connected to what they are learning in the classroom. Putting that into practice is another matter. It's one of the ongoing challenges school librarians face. At the elementary level, teachers often just want to drop their kids off at the door and pick them up when the library period is over. Middle and high school teachers feel they have no time to work with school librarians.

Changing these attitudes and perceptions is up to you. It takes time. Relationships must be built. Sometimes you end up going forward two small steps and then back one or two. Despite the challenge and occasional setbacks, you persevere because the goal is worth the effort.

One of the six Shared Foundations in the *National School Library Standards for Learners, School Librarians, and School Libraries* (2018) is Collaborate. The Key Commitment is "Works effectively with others to broaden perspectives and works toward common goals."[1] This is an important life skill because in our world people are expected to be able to function as part of a team.

There are two main areas where school librarians need to create collaboration. Although when librarians speak of collaboration, they usually are referring to working with teachers on a research class assignment, it is also important to engage students in collaborative learning activities. The *National School Library Standards* addresses both forms of collaboration. In the Framework for Learners, under Collaboration in the standards for the four Domains and Competencies, it states the expectation that students will work together to solve problems and create new knowledge

The Domains and Competencies for school librarians for the Shared Foundation Collaboration are to facilitate, demonstrate, and promote student participation in a variety of ways. Collaborating with teachers comes under the Domains and Alignments for school libraries. Here is where you are expected to develop these to "partner with other educators" in "leading inquiry-based learning opportunities" as well as "demonstrating and reinforcing that information is a shared resource."[2]

COLLABORATING WITH STUDENTS

Engaging students in collaborative projects is the easier aspect of collaboration, but it is not as simple as you may think. Yes, kids naturally play together, but schoolwork is different. Schools historically required students to work on their own, and not copy from anyone else. In schools where parents are active, some are concerned that other children may receive credit for the work their children did. Despite those throwbacks to the past, you need to have students work collaboratively.

Kindergarten– Grade 2

Students in grades K–2 are not ready to work productively with too many others. To get them accustomed to collaborating, you can have them do pair/shares. For example, after you read a story, give students one or two minutes for one student to tell a partner something related to a question you pose. Then the roles are reversed.

After both students have shared with each other, have them report back what they learned. Then have the pairs ask each other a question they would like to know based on the story. Alternatively, they can draw a picture together to show what they learned from each other.

When you search online for library lessons, evaluate them carefully. A clever use of technology doesn't make a lesson good. It may make it fun, but technology should serve as a tool, not a goal. Worksheets that require only one right answer do not develop critical thinking no matter how pretty they look. Remember, if an answer can be found on Google, it doesn't require critical thinking.

A common favorite lesson is learning about the parts of the book. This has been around for over fifty years. As discussed, lessons should have an essential question. Why do students need to know this? If you can't answer the question, don't teach it.

With the essential question in mind, create a class book. Each student or pair of students can work on one page. With a typical sized class, you could do an alphabet book (but you will need to help with those difficult letters). As they put the book together, they will learn about the parts of a book. Add it to your catalog, and let students know how they can then find it.

Another possible lesson is for students to learn where to find out more about the people who created a book so they can borrow more titles by that author or illustrator. A future lesson would teach how to cite a source.

Grades 3–5

In grades 3–5, students can usually work in groups of three to four. As a group, they generate their questions and determine what they will explore. Then have them divide the project into tasks where each one takes responsibility for a specific part. A checklist to help them stay focused and on task should include these steps. They are to indicate who did what as part of their finished work. This allows you to assess the product both individually and collectively.

Design lessons that require movement. At this age, the students are still not good at sitting for long stretches. Use whiteboards or dry erase paper you can put on tabletops, which gives them the opportunity to walk around the table and make contributions. If each group member has a different-colored marker, you can easily assess individuals' contributions.

You, too, should be in motion. Move from group to group as students are working. observe their progress and how they work through problems. This is feedback that will give you the information you need to tweak the assignment in the future. When you recognize a group has lost their way or gone off track, ask guiding questions to get them back to the task at hand.

Middle School

Creating the groups for middle school can be problematic. Although middle school students enjoy group activity, they don't necessarily like working with everyone in their class. If you give students the option of picking their groups, one or two unpopular students are likely to be left out. If you assign groups, you are apt to hear, "Do we have to work with them?"

Preparation will prevent this problem most of the time. Let them know you are going to be putting them in groups and tell them they are not necessarily going to have only their friends in the group. Explain that they are expected to include all members of their group when working together. In some instances, group dynamics can be part of the grade.

Despite your best efforts, you may still find one member of the group is ostracized by others. Handle this quietly. Remind the group about what you said. Do not let them get into the reasons why they dislike this one person. Instead have them come up with ways to get along and accomplish the task at hand.

High School

High school students have become comfortable with group projects. They still may not like working with someone, so you will need to be alert to when it's time to step in. The group size can be larger, which also tends to mitigate the problem.

Groups at this level are often formed based on the topic chosen. Sometimes students work individually on one aspect of their project, making sure to keep track of citations so one group member can compile the combined bibliography. As a group, they will decide how to organize their final presentation, the apps or web resources they will use, and any media they will add.

COLLABORATING WITH TEACHERS

When collaborating with teachers, several levels come into play. Most often we discuss the cooperative and collaborative processes, but there are two stages that come before the cooperative and one after the collaborative stage. The *Learning Commons* website defines the approaches this way:

- *Controlled (isolated approach)*. Everyone works on their own agendas often without knowledge of each other's talents and expertise.
- *Connected (outreach approach)*. The teacher sends students to the library for resources and the teacher librarian pulls together resources to send to the classroom.
- *Cooperative (invitational approach)*. The teacher invites the teacher-librarian to add value to the teacher's assignment (e.g., by teaching search skills) or the teacher-librarian develops an invitational lesson (e.g., by providing book talks).
- *Collaborative (deliberate approach)*. Both teachers partner to co-design, teach, and assess a learning experience that infuses "high think," information literacy, and technology boosts.
- *Creative co-teaching (responsive approach)*. All teachers and specialists work together in the learning commons to provide self-directed discovery and project learning experiences that are in tune with evolving technology opportunities, knowledge environments and learner's interests and needs.[3]

Most elementary librarians and some middle school librarians have a fixed schedule that's usually handed to them by their principal. Many see one class after another, which barely leaves time to set up for the next class. Just finding time to get books returned and shelved is difficult. Working collaboratively with a teacher can seem virtually impossible. Far too many remain at the level of "controlled."

If you never work with teachers, they will not know what you do. If they don't know what you do, they will see no value to your program beyond keeping their kids busy while they have a free period. This is what, in my opinion, contributed to so many library positions being eliminated.

Remember, principals invariably were teachers first. Their assessment of the value of librarians is often based on their experiences as teachers. It is essential you find ways to connect with teachers. Some will become principals.

For an elementary librarian, collaboration may be impossible. Certainly, it can't occur immediately. But you can teach cooperatively. To do so, you must know what is happening in the classroom.

Eating lunch with teachers is a good way to begin. You may have been getting clerical work done while wolfing down your lunch but building relationships with teachers is more important. Listen to what they are talking about. Learn who they are as people and find out what unit is coming up next in their classes. See if you can get a copy of the curriculum for the different grades and any time line teachers are to follow.

Armed with this information, look for resources that can help the teacher or lessons you can do when their students come to the library. Resources include books, apps, and websites. AASL's Best Digital Tools for Teaching and Learning are a treasure trove of resources that you can find on the AASL website.

While working on building relationships with teachers, send an e-mail to the ones with whom you are making connections. Include a link to a relevant resource and an offer to show how to use it. Don't push. Just keep working on building your relationship. If you have a lesson that coordinates with what is being taught in a class, let the teacher know what you are planning to do. Don't blindside the teacher, who may not want you to detract from what is going on in the class. If this doesn't work with one teacher, it may work with another.

Teachers may resist collaboration, but when it occurs, they discover its worth. I did one lesson for a science teacher who agreed to let me do it as a "favor." Not only was the student product superior, but they also found the learning had a positive effect on assignments throughout the rest of the year. The following year, they asked me to do a three-day lesson on science research.

Another science teacher and I worked on a unit on recycling. When the formative assessment showed the students hadn't gotten the full idea of how to select relevant material, they brought the class back, and I focused on how to do so. The results were what they were looking for. The following year, we repeated the lesson, building on what we had learned. My experiences are backed up by a research study conducted by David V. Loertscher.[4]

The challenge is convincing a teacher to let you do that first lesson. Keep trying, but don't inundate them. The teachers are already overstressed. You are there to help, not add to their load. Cooperation comes slowly. As teachers tentatively try your suggestions, trust is built. And from there you can do more together. You may never achieve collaboration, but the teachers will value your contribution.

Libraries that move into being learning commons promote collaboration just by their physical structure. They have areas that foster different types of learning experiences. One is for the solitary learner or reader. The second is a social space that can accommodate gaming, a makerspace, or group work.

The third area is meant for collaboration. It is flexibly designed so furniture can be easily rearranged. The message it sends is a powerful one for serious collaboration. The level of work produced here entices more teachers to want to work in that environment.

Explore Learning commons to see what you like best and what would be a realistic possibility for your school. Try to incorporate those elements into your current library. Armed with the results, develop a plan to turn your library into a learning commons to present to your principal. You will never know what you can achieve unless you try.

Middle and High Schools

In most middle and all high schools, you have no set schedule. Classes come to you with the teachers who sign up to bring them to the library. How often this occurs will, at first, depend on your predecessor. If the previous librarian had been proactive and built a strong program, you will inherit that. It will be up to you to maintain and grow it. On the other hand, if there was little or no outreach to teachers, you will have to work hard to create the program you want.

You will always have some teachers signing up for the library, even if they don't want you to do anything other than make the space available to them. When they do schedule their class, ask what the assignment is. Offer a specific service such as showing students the databases they will need for their work. Try to ascertain what the essential questions are for the project. If the teacher seems open, offer suggestions about how the project might be made more inquiry-based.

Work on building relationships with those teachers with whom you feel a connection before trying to get them to collaborate with you. Learn who they are as people. Actively listen to discover what they enjoy and learn about their goals for their students. Send them links to websites and articles you think will interest them. Don't bury them. Once a week is enough.

Eventually, you should get to know all the teachers, even in large high schools. Unlike teachers, who can choose to ignore a colleague they dislike, you must have a working relationship with everyone. The library is there to welcome all, and you are the face of the library.

A successful collaboration breeds more collaborations. It starts with the teacher doing the introduction, perhaps in the classroom, with you adding your part when the students come to the library. The teacher quietly observes. As soon as you can, move on to situations where the teacher works with you in the library.

Co-teaching is the ultimate goal. At this level both of you work together from planning through teaching to the final assessment. You probably won't ever be sharing a classroom with a teacher, but after your joint planning session, you might be present when the assignment is introduced. If your schedule precludes you going to the class, the whole project can take place in the library.

Promote the collaboration in its various stages in your reports and on your website, giving credit to the teacher and students. This will raise the interest of other teachers. Keep building relationships. Offer to give ten-minute workshops at department meetings. You may be turned down at first, but as teachers begin to work with you, you will be given opportunities to contribute your expertise.

Multiple Schools

For quite a while, elementary librarians have been assigned to two or more schools. The schools may serve different student levels. It is not uncommon to work in a middle school and a high school or a middle school and an elementary one.

Working in different libraries with completely different groups of teachers and students is a challenge. Add some quirky schedules (e.g., one week it's three days in one school and two in the other, the following week it's two in the first school and three in the second). If you haven't experienced this, you don't realize how stressful this can be.

As you prepare for your day in a given school, mentally close out whatever is transpiring in your other school(s). Focus on what is in front of you. Keep a calendar in whatever digital format you prefer so you don't lose track of your schedules and commitments in each of your locations.

Although some of you may have schools at the same level, others may be assigned to one K–2 school and a grade 3–5 school. This may feel like having one large elementary school, but each part has a different culture and feel. On the one hand, having a range of student grade levels makes for more interesting lessons. But it also means you can't use the same lessons in both schools.

Multiple-school assignments are increasingly happening in middle and high schools. It's most common for a librarian to have two middle schools or a middle school and a high school. Although on the surface this may appear to be similar to being assigned to multiple elementary schools, the challenges are even greater.

Because elementary librarians assigned to multiple schools have a fixed schedule, they do get to see students regularly, if not nearly as often as would be ideal. At the secondary level, being split between two buildings severely reduces the time available to build relationships and get teachers and classes into the library. And an empty library suggests there doesn't need to be a librarian. Somehow you must find a way to build the relationships that will lead to collaboration.

Focus your attention on a handful of teachers who seem most likely to work with you. When you give orientations at the start of the year, be mindful of the teachers, how they respond to you, and how they work with their students. This will help guide you about how to make contact.

Try e-mailing a teacher in advance of your next scheduled time in the building to set up a ten-minute conference. If the teacher is willing, you have your foot in the door and can propose a mini research project. Set up the lesson, essential question and all. E-mail it to the teacher for changes and modifications.

Celebrate every connection you make. Making progress in slow steps takes patience, but you are heading in the right direction. You are also demonstrating your value.

There is one other challenge with multiple schools. You have more than one principal. Each administrator has a different way of running the school and, as a result, each school has a different climate. The principals will each have different expectations for the library program. Schedule a meeting to learn what they want, and what their school goals are. Your job will be to show how your library program will advance those goals. Remember—these are their goals, not yours. You can always fit your goals to theirs.

If possible, meet with your principals before the start of the school year. Share your mission and vision for the school library. Ask what their expectations are. How would they describe a highly effective school library? You may not agree with their views, and, if so, you will need to work on modifying it. But you must do what you can to meet each administrator's aims—no matter how different they are from each other.

When you feel that you have made the principals (or even just one principal) aware of who you are, share the School Library Evaluation Checklist from the *National School Library Standards*.[5] You are probably not doing all the things listed, mainly because of how your time is divided and how much your budget is. However, it becomes a good conversation starter that shows what you are trying to achieve and why.

A word about school and district cultures. Every district's culture is different and to a great extent so is every school's. Culture is dependent on a variety of influences ranging from socioeconomic status to local history.

Everything from how discipline is handled to the perception of the library and the openness to innovation rests on culture. A school's culture is frequently affected by the principal, but it takes a while for the impact to be felt. In these days of rapid administrative turnover, school culture can be a muddle.

Your planning should always take the school's culture into consideration. Frame what you want to do in a way that's aligned with that culture. Do you want a green wall? If the school culture is against innovation, you need to show how it fits into current work. On the other hand, should the culture embrace the new, explain what exciting things the kids will be able to do once it's in the library.

To discover the culture in your building, be aware of how teachers in general interact with students. What is their overall attitude towards the principal and central administration? Do the complainers outnumber the supporters? Although you can never make negative comments nor repeat what you hear—good or bad—recognize how these factors come together to form the culture. When you are building your relationships, start with those teachers who have a positive outlook.

AIDES AND VOLUNTEERS

The library program generates a great deal of clerical work, including checking books in and out, shelving them, and processing new acquisitions as well as numerous other tasks. Aides are a vanishing breed, although if you work in multiple schools you may have one at each. At the elementary level you may have parent volunteers to help out. In some places you may have student volunteers. Are these assistants a help or a challenge? The answer is: it depends.

In the best of all possible worlds, extra pairs of hands are a welcome addition. They free you up to teach classes, work with individual students, help teachers learn about tech resources to integrate into their teaching, and fulfill your many other professional responsibilities and roles. Parent volunteers can be your best advocates in the community. They tell others about the learning going on in the library. They go to Board of Education meetings if any cuts are being planned.

Unfortunately, you don't always live in the best of all possible worlds. Although paid clerks/aides/paras (or whatever they are called in your district) have become rare, some prove to be a thorn in the librarian's side. Because they have been there longer, they may assume that they know more than you do. In some cases, they may discipline students, override a decision you make, or intentionally help out teachers to imply they are more capable than the new librarian. (The same can be true of volunteers.)

You cannot allow yourself to be bullied but being angry and argumentative will only exacerbate the situation. Sit down with the bully and have a talk, perhaps over coffee. Let them know how much you value their help and input.

Acknowledge that they are more familiar with the teachers, the routines, and the collection than you are and because of that knowledge you are counting on their help.

Once you have outlined their contributions, explain that much as you appreciate what they bring, you need them to give you room to be the librarian. You will get to know the teachers, the routines, and the collection soon enough. You rely on them to make it all possible, by taking care of the clerical tasks that you now oversee.

Find out if there is something the aide particularly likes doing, such as creating displays and bulletin boards. Give them this responsibility, and then point out their work to teachers and the principal. Make sure you let them see that you value their contributions and recognize how they help the library program flourish.

Volunteers can be as problematic as an aide who believes they know more than you. Parents of young students like opportunities to see their child at work. Their help is great, but unfortunately they also bring challenges. They must immediately be trained in library procedures. Many don't know how to shelve according to the Dewey Decimal System or whatever system you are using. Checking books in and out using your automated system is new to them. Create a Google doc or other method to keep track of their training and have them sign off on what they have completed.

In addition to not knowing library routines, volunteers' behavior can also cause problems. Begin by welcoming and thanking them for volunteering. Every volunteer should receive a list of expectations that include showing up on the day and time they are scheduled or informing you as soon as possible if they can't make it. They should know whether you will permit younger children to accompany them. Their cell phones should be on vibrate and any calls are to be taken in the library office.

If volunteers cover your library when you are at your other school, also carefully spell out what they can't do. One librarian I know discovered that the volunteers had relabeled and shelved books and moved chapter books in with picture books. Because many of these were shorter than the majority of books, it wasn't easy to find them, especially because the records hadn't been changed.

Although volunteers can be your biggest boosters in the community, they can cause problems by sharing information that should be confidential. Parents must recognize that what happens in the library, stays in the library. They cannot gossip about individual students reveal what they read, or how they behave. They also should not make negative observations about teachers while they are in the library. You can't prevent it from happening, but by bringing these rules to their attention, you reduce the number of incidents.

Create a volunteer manual that covers all important information. Open with a welcoming greeting, thanking them for their help. As with your student rules, frame your expectations positively. The manual should reflect your philosophy, mission, and vision.

Use a Google form for volunteers to indicate they have read the manual. Also provide a training session to give them hands-on information. We all learn best by doing. Update the manual to add information you might have missed the first time or to include changes made to the library.

High schools and most middle schools don't as a rule have parent volunteers but may have student volunteers. School library aides at the upper elementary level can be extremely helpful; in general, fourth to sixth graders tend to be very conscientious.

You can tap older students who want to show volunteer work on their college applications. Some do it because they love libraries. However, just like you, they will get bored if all they are doing is shelving. To keep them interested, assign your library aides their own shelves. They can shelve books in their area and keep the books in order. Give them some guidelines for weeding and have them bring you any titles they think meet those criteria.

For a time, I had student helpers who were assigned to the library to make up for a class they had failed. They weren't motivated, and I would look for activities that they would find somewhat interesting. One way to motivate and reward them is by giving them digital badges. By acknowledging their work, you are apt to improve the quality of it, even for students who have been unwillingly assigned to the library.

Parent and student aides can also create bulletin boards and displays. If you are not particularly artistic, this can be a great help. Show them ideas you have seen on Pinterest or on library related Facebook pages to get them started. Be sure to give them credit by posting a tag reading, "Created by ___."

Your clerk or volunteers also must be mindful of not disrupting any teaching you are doing. Unlike a classroom where one thing is happening at a time even if students are working at centers, in the library several types of activities are often going on simultaneously. While you are teaching and interacting with students, you must also stay aware of whatever else is happening.

All your volunteers should acquire new skills from their work. If you teach them search techniques, older students can create webliographies for teachers or perform similar tasks. Parents, too, can become skilled at cybersafety and identifying misinformation on the internet.

🛡 KEY IDEAS

- Students learn more when library lessons are connected to what is happening in the classroom.
- Getting teachers to work with you is challenging on every level. With a fixed schedule, they may only want to leave their students and pick them up when the period is over. In a flex schedule, they feel they are too busy to take their classes to the library.

- Although you need to develop approaches that will connect you to the classroom, you also need to incorporate collaboration in your lessons, teaching students how to work together effectively.
- K–2 students can learn to work together doing pair/share exercises.
- Avoid worksheets that require a single right answer—and therefore very little thinking.
- Grades 3–5 can work in groups of three to four.
- Covering tables with dry erase paper allows students to walk around their work, adding needing movement to the lesson.
- Move from group to group as they work so you can get immediate feedback on how they are progressing and where they might be struggling.
- Be prepared for middle school students to object to someone being assigned to their group.
- High school groups can be larger and may be formed based on the topic chosen.
- Collaboration between school librarians and teachers ranges from the controlled (no contact) level to creative co-teaching.
- Eating lunch with teachers can help you discover what they are teaching and give you an opportunity to reach out to them.
- Build opportunities for collaboration by exploring the possibility of converting your library into a learning commons.
- Get copies of the different curriculums and look for websites and other resources that connect to them. Share your findings with teachers and offer your help.
- When middle and high school teachers schedule their classes into the library but don't want your help, ask what the assignment is and offer a specific service such as teaching about a relevant database.
- Ask about essential questions, and if the teacher is open, suggest how the project can be more inquiry-based.
- Build relationships before suggesting collaborating.
- Successful collaboration breeds more collaboration, and others who see the results are more likely to work with you.
- Acknowledge the teachers who work with you in your reports to the administration.
- Offer to give brief presentations at department or grade level meetings.
- School librarians assigned to multiple schools need to keep track of what is happening in each building and focus only on the one they are at for the day.
- When you have a flex schedule and are at multiple schools make connections as soon as possible with the teachers who seem most willing to work with you.

- E-mail one of those supportive teachers in advance of your next scheduled time in that building and try to set up a ten-minute meeting to plan a small project.
- Multiple schools mean multiple principals, each with different expectations for the library program.
- Schedule a meeting with each principal, preferably in the summer, to learn their expectations and share your mission and vision.
- When you have made a connection with a principal, give them a copy of the School Library Evaluation Checklist and explain how you will be working to fulfill them.
- Every district and school has its own culture. Understanding it and framing your plans to align with it will make you more successful.
- Aides and volunteers can be helpful or challenging.
- Parent volunteers can be your biggest advocates.
- Aides who have been in the library before you were hired may think they know more than you and take on professional tasks.
- Improve your relationship with an aide by learning which tasks they like best and praising their contributions.
- Be welcoming to and appreciative of volunteers but be sure to establish your expectations for them.
- Train volunteers in library procedures and ensure they understand the importance of protecting student privacy.
- Give student aides opportunities beyond tasks like shelving by asking them to create bulletin boards, displays, and even webliographies.
- Make sure there is value for the volunteers in giving their time and work.

NOTES

1. American Association of School Librarians, 2018, *National School Library Standards for Learners, School Librarians, and School Libraries,* 84.
2. AASL, *National School Library Standards,* 85.
3. "Collaboration and Coteaching," *Learning Commons,* www.schoollearning commons.info/making-it-work/collaboration-and-coteaching.
4. David V. Loertscher, "Collaboration and Coteaching: A New Measure of Impact," *Teacher Librarian* 42 (2), https://docs.google.com/viewer?a=v&pid=sites&srcid =ZGVmYXVsdGRvbWFpbnxzY2hvb2xsZWFybmluZ2NvbW1vbN8Z3g6Mz U3NTFlZjQ2NTI1YThlNQ.
5. AASL, School Library Evaluation Checklist, American Association of School Librarians, https://standards.aasl.org/wp-content/uploads/2018/10/180921 -aasl-standards-evaluation-checklist-color.pdf.

5
The Curriculum

In the preceding chapters, we have discussed lesson plans and collaboration. What is a straightforward matter for classroom teachers can be complex, and occasionally convoluted, for librarians. Curriculum presents even more challenges for school librarians.

A curriculum is a compilation of the knowledge and skills students are expected to learn. It is generally broken down into grade levels and content areas and gives the learner outcomes or objectives for large concepts as well as individual units. It may specify what materials and texts are to be used and how it is to be implemented.

The curriculum is connected to standards. It identifies the state standards to be addressed as well as subject area standards for the content being covered. Additionally, a curriculum should spell out how the learning outcomes are to be assessed. Many curriculums also include benchmarks and pacing guides specifying the time allotted to each unit. When essential questions are part of the curriculum, they direct the structure and content of the units.

As a point of interest, many educators talk about three types of curriculums: the stated curriculum, the hidden curriculum, and the absent curriculum. The *stated curriculum* is what is given to teachers and is sometimes posted on the school's website. The *hidden curriculum* is what is taught as the teacher implements the stated curriculum.

The *absent curriculum* is what is not included, either purposefully or accidentally. Sometimes teachers' own biases may be why they ignore some aspects of a subject. For example, climate change and evolution are two topics that are in the hidden curriculum in different parts of the country. Sex education courses may only offer abstinence as the means of preventing contraception.

On a lighthearted note, it used to be said that the stated or official curriculum was what was put in a teacher's drawer. The hidden curriculum was what was taught. Although closer monitoring has meant that the stated curriculum is addressed most of the time, individual creativity, student needs, and class composition are reasons that the hidden curriculum is still in place.

For librarians in many locations, the hidden curriculum is all they teach. The first challenge you may face is that not every district has a library curriculum, even when they have a librarian. This doesn't mean you should wing it. You should know where you are going, why you are going there, and how you will know if your got there. That requires a curriculum, even if it's only sketched out.

At whatever level you are working, with or without a library curriculum, you must obtain the curriculums for what is being taught in the classroom. As an elementary librarian who functions at the controlled level of collaboration (see chapter 4), you can still make an impact if you know what is happening in the classroom. The curriculums will give you that information.

If the curriculum has a pacing guide, you can anticipate when specific material will be taught, which will give your lessons more relevance to classroom lessons. Share what you have done with teachers. It can lead to working more cooperatively but be prepared for blowback from some teachers who will feel you are invading their territory. Should that occur, look for lessons that mirror or complement class work without impinging on what is taught in the classroom.

Flexibly scheduled librarians should ask for copies of all subject and grade level curriculums as well. This is part of the challenge you face. See where research activities would give greater depth to a unit and offer to create a project with the teacher. Plan on doing most, if not all, of the work.

Teachers have a defined number of curriculums to deal with. Elementary and some middle school teachers are concerned only with the subject areas for their grade. High school teachers have a curriculum for their subject and the levels of it they teach. You deal with all of it. Although it's a challenge, the more familiar you are with the teachers' curriculums, the better you will be able to initiate collaborative projects.

The curriculums should connect to the appropriate state standards for the subject and grade. Additionally, they should include any national standards such as those for language arts, social studies, and STEM. Your designated curriculum—or the one you develop—should include these as well as AASL's *National School Library Standards for Learners, School Librarians, and School Libraries*. When you create your lessons, you need to be mindful of all these standards.

CREATING A CURRICULUM

If you look at a number of curriculums, it is immediately obvious that they vary widely in detail and complexity. Should you be assigned a curriculum, obviously you must follow it. You may notice there are many gaps in it, particularly in connection to what is happening in the classrooms. This is when you need to use the hidden curriculum. In other words, make additions as needed.

If you aren't given a curriculum you need to develop one. To begin, review the school library curriculums available online. As you explore them, select what will work for you, your students, teachers, and school.

EXAMPLES OF CURRICULUMS

Four examples illustrate the differences among curriculums. In analyzing their strengths and weaknesses, you will see their commonalities as well as their dissimilarities. The similarities tell you what must be included, although how you present it will vary. The differences are where you will make your own choices.

To show this contrast more sharply, we will look at two district-level curriculums and two state-level ones. As you might expect, the district ones are simpler and have been prepared by local librarians. Despite being done locally, both are long. They still cite the old AASL standards. But if you were using either curriculum, you could easily take what is there and plug in the new standards.

The purpose of unpacking the four curriculums is to help you deal with their intricacies from the simplest (which isn't that simple) to the most complex. This is intended to serve as guide to help you walk through the different parts and take away what you consider most valuable.

District-Level Curriculum: The Morris School District

The Morris School District (New Jersey) has an elementary curriculum for K–5 and another one for its high school. Currently there is no curriculum for middle school.

All six elementary curricula follow the same arrangement, which is posted online.[1] For example, the online calendar for the grade 3 information literacy unit shows a time line. The first column lists the units of study. Bars indicate the months in which they are taught. Clicking on the title of a unit will take you to a screen listing enduring understandings, essential questions, concepts (what students will know), skills and performance expectations (what students will be able to do), and the targeted New Jersey and national standards.

For example, the essential questions for the grade 3 research unit are:

- What is the research process?
- How can I research and gather information ethically to avoid plagiarism?
- Where can students find relevant and authoritative information?
- How can students organize and present their information through use of technology?
- When researching information, what criteria should be in place for evaluating trustworthy websites?
- How can I effectively research information on the Google search engine to make a research topic manageable?
- What is the difference between fact and opinion? What is biased material?
- How am I displaying the qualities of digital citizenship?

The concepts (what students will know with assistance from the media specialist) are:

- How to read informational texts for lifelong learning.
- How to evaluate websites for credibility and trustworthiness.
- How to effectively use the process for research.
- The difference between fact and opinion.
- How to express information in own words and abide with copyright laws.
- How to use basic Google search operators.
- How to present research information digitally through Google Suite for Education.
- Which domain endings are best for researching information.

Following the same structure, the unit on the Ethical Use of Information and Technology at the high school level lists these essential questions:[2]

- How do we use information ethically?
- How do we interact with information safely?
- How do we use information productively in a global society?

The concepts for the unit are:

- Avoid bias by using a wide variety of sources.

- Recognize that many issues have differing viewpoints.
- Know when to cite and how to use standard citation formatting.
- Use proper netiquette when using technology and information resources both in school and in personal situations.

You are not given any idea of content for these units. However, the units have enough information for you to determine what you want to achieve. Librarians can create their own lesson plans or find ones online that match the content.

District-Level Curriculum: The Tri-District Library/Information Literacy Curriculum

The Tri-District Library/Information Literacy Curriculum begins with its mission statement and philosophy.[3] This forms an excellent basis for the curriculum (although I wish it also included a vision statement). It next lists the Common Beliefs of the 2007 *AASL Standards* The many roles of the school librarian are then listed, including what they encompass.

The curriculum then begins with the first unit for K–2. For each unit you are given:

- state standards
- big ideas/common threads
- enduring understandings
- essential questions
- module assessment
- lesson objectives
- module skills

The same structure is used for all levels through high school. A list of resources concludes all units of study through grade 8. For the high school, the curriculum lists resources by standard.

This is followed by Information Literacy Curriculum Content Standards and Student Objectives Grades 7–12. For each of them you are given what is an essential question for the standard, an objective, and where students should be at the end of grade 8 and grade 12. Appendix B presents the state standards (which, because of when this was written, are the Common Core Curriculum Standards). Appendix C is the old AASL Standards, *Empowering Learners: Guidelines for School Library Programs* (2009).[4] Appendix D is the Tri-District K-6 Library/Information Literacy Curriculum Matrix.

The two sample state-level curriculums contain far more content. The one created by the Pennsylvania School Library Association is intended to assist librarians who either don't have a curriculum or want to modify the existing curriculum.

State-Level Curriculum: The Pennsylvania School Library Association Model Curriculum

The Pennsylvania School Library Association Model Curriculum is structured as a framework to guide school librarians in partnering with teachers and meeting the Pennsylvania Core Standards for ELA. The first section is an overview followed by three parts:[5]

The overview explains how the model curriculum is structured. (Additionally, the Overview has two approaches to using the model curriculum, and a list of resources including those for understanding by design and academic and literacy standards.) Stage 1 is "Desired Results," which include the essential questions and the correlations with the Pennsylvania Core Standards. Stage 2 gives the assessment evidence used to indicate whether students exhibit the desired results. Stage 3 is the learning plan, which uses the Understanding by Design model to design the lessons.

After explaining the alignment with the Pennsylvania Core Standards, Stage 1 focuses on desired results. It begins with the long-term transfer goals, which are, in essence, equivalent to enduring understandings. Below this are two columns for the six big ideas and the essential questions. Big ideas are then color-coded into seven clusters:

- effective readers
- critical thinkers
- active listeners
- effective speakers
- effective research
- audience and purpose
- responsible citizens

A color-coded table gives concepts for each big idea.

This is followed by the essential questions for each big idea along with the concepts that are derived from it along with appropriate standards. Stage 1 concludes with a summary giving the total number of competencies by grade level for each of the big ideas. The addition of the big idea gives a larger context to the essential questions. Not every curriculum has this, but it's something you might want to consider including in your own curriculum

Part 2 continues Stage 1, the desired results for the library information concepts. The big ideas are given along with the essential questions, followed by a table for the library that uses color-coded bands to indicate the grade ranges for each of the concepts, the competencies, and the various standards. You have the option of choosing to focus on one grade band.

Part 3 of the Model Curriculum deals with Stage 3—Assessments and Learning Plan. It gives the template for the GRASPS model: **G**oal; **R**ole; **A**udience; **S**ituation; **P**roduct/Performance and Purpose; and **S**tandards and Criteria for Success. The acronym is one worth considering in designing your curriculum and its assessments.

A sample of a GRASPS assessment follows.

The learning plan gives specific unit topics for each cluster, color banded by grade and divided into columns for the big idea it deals with. An alternative arrangement is offered for the different performance tasks with a column for the big idea, its library information concepts, and a column for each grade band.

To create lesson plans, the Model Curriculum uses the acronym *WHERETO*. *WHERE* stands for:

- Where? What? Why?
- Hook and hold to engage students.
- Explore, experience, enable, equip.
- Rethink, revise, rehearse, refine.
- Evaluate work and progress.

TO is about focusing the lesson plan:

- Tailor and personalize for all students.
- Organize and sequence for optimal effectiveness (cover and uncover).

Further help is provided with a page of instructional strategies and three templates: one for WHERETO, another for sequenced instructional strategies and student learning experiences, and yet another for listing different types of resources supporting the lesson plan.

Additionally, there are sample lesson plans and supplements for each grade band. These are completely filled out using the templates, and address the big ideas, essential questions, and learning concepts.

This is an extensive curriculum that offers a great deal of support for librarians. Although a librarian can go through it as I just did to understand its arrangement, its contents, and where to find things, it will take time to feel fully comfortable with it. The best approach is to focus on a grade band you serve in your school and follow it all the way through.

State-Level Curriculum: The Empire State Information Fluency Curriculum

The Empire State Information Fluency Curriculum (ESIFC) is the second state-level curriculum we'll explore.[6] This is New York State's curriculum, based on the one developed for New York City. It is modeled on the six phases of Barbara Stripling's Cycle of Inquiry and Learning, which has six phases: connect, wonder, investigate, construct, express, and reflect, and then back to connect again in this continuing cycle.[7]

Publication of the new standards required an update to ESIFC. The website shows the work in progress as well as the ESIFC itself. For an overall view of the document, go to the website and click on Digital Copy of the ESIFC. Choose Table of Contents, which lists the seven sections. Taking them one at a time will allow you to slowly assimilate the different sections of the curriculum.

Section 1 presents the frameworks, giving the four Anchor Standards with explanations: inquiry and design thinking, multiple literacies, social and civic responsibility, and personal growth and agency.

Section 2 is the PK–12 Continuum itself, along with the appropriate Priority Skills for the three Anchor Standards. For example, this is the Anchor Standard 1 for grades 3–5:

> Anchor Standard I—Inquiry and Design Thinking: Use Inquiry and Design Thinking to Build Understanding and Create New Knowledge. We are thinkers and designers. Standard 1.1: Information-fluent learners use an inquiry process to connect to prior experience and background knowledge, wonder and ask questions, investigate, construct new understanding, express learning, and reflect on the process and product of learning.

Section 3 contains the Priority Skills. By focusing solely on these, you can see how they develop over the grade levels. There is an overview for grades PK–12, which then breaks then down into the usual grade bands. For example, this is the Priority Skill for Connect and Anchor Standard 1 for grades 3–5:

> CONNECT 3-5 Priority Skills Interest and Prior Knowledge
> - Identifies aspects of the broad topic that would be important and interesting to pursue through inquiry Background and Key Words
> - Uses a source provided by the teacher to acquire background information
> - Generates a list of key words for a research-based project with guidance

Section 4 is a twelve-page printable brochure intended for use by teachers, administrators, and parents that is also an excellent resource in structuring a curriculum and planning lessons.

Section 5 has assessments by grade. There are assessments for each of the Priority Skills at every grade level ranging from four for PK to forty for grades 9–10. To see these assessments, go to IFC Downloads after Section 7.

Section 6 is the Assessment by Standard. It contains all the graphic organizers by standard so that, "if you are teaching a skill during the Investigate phase of inquiry, for example, you will be able to browse through all of the graphic organizers for Investigate and then adopt or adapt any organizer that matches your lesson." As with Section 5 you will need to go the IFC Downloads to see them. Choose the documents you want to in advance as the download is 313 pages. There are handouts to print out and use for your assessment. For example, on "connecting ideas to own interests," the student is to fill in four "I want to find out" bubbles surrounding "ideas I heard." These handouts go on for pages, becoming more complex as they move on through the grade levels.

Section 7 is *REACTS*, an acronym for a taxonomy that describes the six levels of research reactions, which also align with Bloom's taxonomy.

- **R**ecalling—Level 1
- **E**xplaining—Level 2
- **A**nalyzing—Level 3
- **C**hallenging—Level 4
- **T**ransforming—Level 5
- **S**ynthesizing—Level 6

Sample assignments are given for all the levels along with a list of action words to use for each one.

Sharon Fox, a librarian in Orange County, New York, has done librarians a great service by designing a template for creating lessons using the current AASL Standards. Although she designed the Google Sheet Template for New York school librarians to use with the Continuum, she is freely offering it to everyone.[8]

Begin with the file "How to Use," and then check out the FAQs. Explore the other files on AASL lesson plans and sample lesson plans. This is an outstanding way to organize and keep track of your teaching as well as sharing with other librarians in your district and beyond. You might set this up for your own state.

Obviously, the ESIFC is enormous. It takes time to work your way through it, but it is well organized and worth looking at. It shows how information literacy—or information fluency, as New York calls it, is built over the years.

An important takeaway from the analysis of the four curriculums is they are not static. All of them need to be reassessed and updated periodically. It will take a while before all the curriculums incorporate the *National School Library Standards* from AASL. Even without the updating they still are helpful.

Continue to look for examples of school library curriculums online. Many districts have their curriculum as part of Creative Commons licenses or are willing to let you use theirs. If you find yourself on a curriculum writing committee for your district school libraries or for a grade or subject area, use these resources for guidance and for helping you create one that best meets student needs.

CURRICULUM MAPS

A curriculum map is a visual representation of the curriculum. It shows what skills and topics occur at each grade level, indicating what is taught when and how long it should take. The purpose is to identify what should be dropped because a concept or topic has been previously taught and to discover where there are holes that need to be filled. The map usually resembles a spreadsheet.

Curriculum maps are similar in some ways to a scope and sequence in that they both show what is to be taught when. The difference is that the map is designed to show the connections between all areas of the curriculum. Scope and sequence show the objectives and order in which skills are to be taught.[9]

Creating a curriculum map is a group project. Normally, a committee of teachers along with an administrator develop it, frequently during the summer. Curriculum mapping software may be used. There are also many templates available online.

When you learn about plans for a curriculum mapping, try to get on the committee. It can do wonders for your program. Having advance knowledge of the units that will be taught allows you to order the resources students and teachers will need. You also can recommend resources from the library to include in the map, and at the same time let teachers know how you can help them in their instruction.

PROFESSIONAL LEARNING NETWORKS AND OTHER RESOURCES

Think of being faced with one of these curriculums when you are at a new school. Where do you start? Most of you will be the sole librarian in your building. Too many of you will be assigned to more than one school. It's a daunting task if you have to do it on your own but it becomes more manageable with help.

You may be the only librarian in your building, but librarians are most helpful profession. Reach out and you will get the advice and support you need. You may even find a mentor. That person will help you on an immediate level, but no mentor knows everything.

Build your professional learning network. If there are other librarians in the district, they are your first contacts. LM_NET (www.lm-net.info/) is possibly the oldest support system for librarians. It is an electronic discussion list with approximately 16,000 members worldwide.

Search Facebook for library-related groups (including LM_Net's). Helpful groups include Future Ready Librarians, Makerspaces and Participatory Libraries, Hacking School Libraries, and my own School Librarian's Workshop. Ask a question and you will find advice, links, and more from the other librarian members of the group.

Your state library association should have also have a discussion list. Discover the Twitter chats that connect to what you are doing. And then there are the websites of the national associations. AASL (www.ala.org/aasl) has an extensive website that you should explore. See their Best Digital Tools for Teaching and Learning (www.ala.org/aasl/awards/best). It has great resources on advocacy and an ever-growing portal on the *National School Library Standards* (standards.aasl.org).

For an extensive list of resources on topics of interest to school librarians see Resources for School Librarians (https://www.sldirectory.com/). For national and local information skills standards, go to https://www.sldirectory.com/libsf/resf/infoskill.html.

You are not alone. With so many librarians there to help, you're on your way to becoming a superstar librarian. Just reach out.

🗋 KEY IDEAS

- Curriculums define what is to be taught and when.
- They typically include all or some of these: standards, outcomes, objectives or goals, pacing guides, benchmarks, and essential questions.
- Frequently there are three curriculums: the stated (official) curriculum, the hidden (what is taught) curriculum, and the absent (what is purposely omitted) curriculum.
- You may or may not have a library curriculum with which to work.
- Get copies of all curriculums taught in your school.
- Librarians on a fixed schedule can use the curriculums and any pacing guide to anticipate what is being taught and use this information to align their lessons with it.
- Librarians on a flex schedule should identify areas in the curriculum that would be best met by a research project in the library.
- In creating your lessons, you need to address the curriculum for the grade/subject area, the relevant state and national standards, and the *National School Library Standards*.
- Curriculums vary in detail and complexity.
- Analyzing different library curriculums help you to develop or update yours.
- District or school curriculums are less complex than those on the state level, but all of these sources can help you find phrases and wording to include in your own curriculum.
- The curriculums of the Pennsylvania School Library Association and New York's Empire State Information Fluency Curriculum are excellent resources for any curriculum.
- Sharon Fox's Google Sheet Template is an excellent place to find and share lesson plans.
- Curriculum maps provide a visual representation of the curriculum and make it easier to discover what is taught and when.

- Serving on a curriculum mapping committee provides you with an opportunity to prepare resources for what will be taught in classrooms, incorporate library lessons into the curriculum, and demonstrate how you can help teachers.
- Develop personal learning networks using Twitter chats and library-related Facebook groups. With the support from colleagues you won't be alone even if you are the sole librarian in the building.

NOTES

1. Morris School District (New Jersey), "Elementary School: Grade 3; Library Digital Literacy," https://morrisschooldistrict-public.rubiconatlas.org/Atlas/Browse/View/UnitCalendar?BackLink=33913&CurriculumMapID=521&YearID=2020&SourceSiteID=.
2. Morris School District (New Jersey), "Unit Planner: Ethical Use of Information Technology," High School: Library/Digital Literacy: MHS Library and Digital Literacy, https://morrisschooldistrict-public.rubiconatlas.org/Atlas/Develop/UnitMap/View/Default?SourceSiteID=&UnitID=15439&YearID=2020&CurriculumMapID=536&.
3. "Tri-District Library/Information Literacy Curriculum, 2011 Grades K – 12," www.riveredgeschools.org/pdf/curriculum/Library%20Curriculum%20K-12.pdf.
4. Association of School Librarians, *Empowering Learners: Guidelines for School Library Programs,* 2009.
5. Pennsylvania School Library Association, "Model Curriculum," 2014, https://www.psla.org/model-curriculum-for-pa-school-library-programs.
6. Empire State Information Fluency Continuum, "LibGuide," 2019, https://slsa-nys.libguides.com/c.php?g=933367&p=6845933&preview=430aaf7ac0b426db97cd7891cf4d7823.
7. "The Stripling Model of Inquiry," https://www.nypl.org/sites/default/files/images/striplingmodel.jpg
8. Sharon Fox, "AASL/ESIFC Lesson Plans," 2019, https://drive.google.com/drive/folders/1PtGJmOJpUAAMXReUzdZANCFczat5yEGU?fbclid=IwAR0MSsMe_ze_pEPWC602NV7T3bhetclDU0aLcRCtCGTJoqz9f6eV0re_39w.
9. Jordan School District (Utah), "The Quick Version of Curriculum Map and Scope and Sequence," http://secondarylanguagearts.jordandistrict.org/files/2015/07/The-Quick-Version-of-Curriculum-Map-and-Scope-and-Sequence.docx.

6
Distractions, Disruptions, and Defiance

On any given school day there will be small and large distractions and disruptions that interfere with the learning process. In the classroom, the minor ones range from students requesting to go to the bathroom to an announcement from the office. These are routine and handled quickly and effortlessly.

Other disruptions, for example lock-down drills, take far more time away from learning. Even when it's over, students don't settle down for a while. Within the library classroom this behavior is magnified. The students are not in their usual space, which exacerbates the situation. If you don't have a plan for these occurrences, it will take even longer to get students settled again. You'll need to remind students they know what to do during a drill. Give them any necessary directions and lead them out, being sure everyone has left.

Know when to go with the flow. As soon as the first snowflake falls, student attention immediately shifts to the windows. If snow begins to fall, your students will almost always lose focus. When snow begins early in the day, they will hope for an early dismissal. Classroom teachers face the same scenario, but it is more contained for the reasons discussed earlier.

Meteorologists have probably forecast the likelihood of snow, so you can anticipate this distraction and prepare for it. For younger students, prepare a snow-related activity. You might read snow stories or poems, have them draw something related to snow, and discuss what causes snow to fall.

At the middle and high school levels, this is harder to deal with. You have a lesson to get through. Determine how distracted students are. If it seems you are really losing them, stop your lesson and ask them to share what they're really working on. How is it going? What successes have they found? Where are they struggling? Encourage feedback from the rest of the class.

DISTRACTIONS AND DISRUPTIONS

In the library setting, distractions also come from students who aren't in your class, teachers, and others. When a teacher closes the door to the classroom, there are few outside interruptions. The library is always open, and people come in and out. These comings and goings are intrusive, some more so than others. Anticipating potential distractions and disruptions will help keep you from being knocked off balance when they occur. You won't be able to predict them, but the philosophy underlying the strategies for dealing with them can usually be put into practice when an unanticipated disturbance occurs.

Students

Students are yours just for the one period, and they don't see you as their "teacher." You don't give them a grade (although you may do so at the elementary level), so many don't feel they have to listen to you. Although grades should not be a reason to pay attention, in reality, it often is. You can offset this at the middle and high school levels by offering to grade students' "Works Cited" pages, for the teachers. This will encourage them to seek you out and listen to what you have to say.

A common disruption is caused by bawdy humor that varies with students' ages. At the lower grade they can become hysterical over the mention of anything related to the bathroom. It's part of the allure of Dav Pilkey's *Captain Underpants* series.

I had a grade 4 student showing some of his classmates the "dirty words" he found in the unabridged dictionary which caused some quiet giggling. One of my volunteers wanted me to intercede. I pointed out the student had to know the word to look it up—and was practicing his dictionary skills.

It becomes a bit more complicated when middle and high school students find nudes in art books. A few librarians have been known to use black marker to cover the offending parts. I don't like the censorship nor the message it sends, which is contrary to what the artist intended to express. I went over to the students and said, "I am surprised. I thought you were old enough to appreciate great art. If you aren't, find something else to do." If you have high school students who still react that way to art books, point out to them that you expected them to be beyond this elementary school silliness.

Be mindful of students at this level who may take advantage of hiding places in the stacks to exchange kisses and more. As discussed in chapter 2, your facility design can help or hinder discipline. This is where a convex mirror can be a preventative.

Obviously, prevention is the best approach. Paying attention to transitions minimize disruptions within the class you are teaching. Ensuring that the lessons engage students is also essential. When you use an inquiry-based approach you give students "choice and voice," which helps them be interested in what they are doing.

But no matter how exciting your lessons are, no matter how warm, friendly, and safe your library space is, there will be students who act out. You need to be prepared for this, so you don't respond from a fight-or-flight mode, but rather have strategies for de-escalating the situation.

The first rule is to remain calm and not raise your voice. The moment students see you are upset—and possibly—fearful, they will take control. Give the students a hard stare or a raised eyebrow to indicate you know what is happening. Keep a sense of humor to lighten the situation. For example, with a smile on your face, you can say, "You made your point, now let's get back to work."

When this doesn't appear to be working, classroom teachers typically will send a student to wait in the hall for a while. This is not necessarily the best response in the library. There is likely to be some incoming traffic and too many ways for the student to get into further trouble. Send the student to another seat away from the rest of the class but still within your view. Have them write or even draw what would have been a better choice. Collect it after about five minutes. You can discuss it later with the student if it seems appropriate.

The same student might repeatedly cause problems. The good thing about this is you will learn their name quickly! On the other hand, you can't permit constant disruptions. Speak with the student's teacher to find out if they behave the same way in class. Also speak privately with the student to try to get at the root of the issue. If all else fails, you need to speak to your administrator.

For some ideas see Linda Shalaway's "Twenty-Five Sure-Fire Strategies for Handling Difficult Students."[1] Although a number of her strategies appear in other sources because they are logical and time-tested, it is helpful when they are collected in one place.

There are many ways students might act out. They have different causes. Try to identify them and adjust your interventions. Here are some possibilities.

Talking

Every class has at least one talker. If you don't deal with a talker, your attention becomes split and you can lose your focus. The talking can be caused by boredom, a student's desire to connect with a friend, or it may just be a bad habit. Check with the class's teacher to find out if this is usual behavior.

Response: Don't tell the student to stop talking. That only calls attention to the behavior. Ask a question related to what the class has been working on. This will bring the student back into the group. If they have lost track of what was happening before the interruption, try some guided questions to elicit a response. You don't want to shame the student in any way. That runs counter to the environment you want to maintain in your library.

Horseplay

Seen most frequently in elementary and middle schools, this ranges from kicking another student while listening to a story, hiding in the stacks during book selection time, or touching another student (sometimes inappropriately at the high school level). Think kids in the back seat during a long ride—and no devices. In older kids this is usually caused by boredom or hormones.

Response: At the elementary and middle school levels, ask the student to identify the rule they are breaking. You want them to acknowledge their behavior rather than wait for you do it. At the high school, say with a small smile, "I know you know better than this. I'm sure you will not do this again."

Zoning Out

Similar to sleeping with eyes open, a zoned-out student may be tired, bored, or possibly drunk or high. The latter can happen at the high school and possibly middle school levels.

Response: Address the student by name to "awaken" your zoned-out sleeper. It's highly unlikely that this student knows what the class has been doing. Ask the them to get something for you. This will give the student time to regain composure. You can also observe whether the student is incapacitated in some way. If that should be the case, contact the nurse or an administrator as soon as possible without disrupting your class. You can probably manage it when students are working in groups.

EVENTS

Fire Drills and Bomb Scares

Although most distractions and disruptions are student-caused, there are others. In addition to lockdowns, fire drills will interrupt your lessons. The challenge for you is to guide the kids outside rather than to their classroom. You also need to know who is supposed to be in the library so you can take attendance once you are outside and again when you return to the library. At the elementary level, take your roster with you. If the teacher is present, they can take charge of their class when you return.

A real fire, which does occur on occasion, works the same way, but you will be outside much longer. The arrival of the fire department adds to the distractions, so avoid getting into conversations with other teachers. You need to keep an eye on your students.

Bomb scares, which are almost never real threats, must be handled like fire drills. Obviously, they are not scheduled in advance. You'll follow the procedure for fire drills.

Drop-Ins—Students

Unlike a classroom, the library is an open space. People come in all the time. Teachers may send students in to take a make-up test in a quiet place, to do some quick research, or to give you a message. Although this is rarer at the elementary level because your activities are usually fully scheduled, it still does happen.

If you are speaking to a class when a drop-in student arrives, signal with your hand to indicate they should wait until you have a break. Once you have students working on a task, you can attend to the drop-in. Be as brief as possible. If more time is necessary, let the student know when you will be free to speak with them.

Drop-ins usually come in after your lesson has begun. Make sure they sign in. If they are resistant to doing this, explain why it is necessary. If there are drop-ins in the library when there is a fire drill, you need to take the sign-in sheet with you.

Students drop in more frequently at the middle and high school levels. In addition to signaling them to wait until you can attend to them, you must be alert for their entrance. Secondary school libraries are larger, and if you are involved with a class you may not notice someone has entered. This gives the drop-in the opportunity to get lost or hide out in the stacks, and later tell the teacher you were too busy to help.

The number of drop-ins increases during lunchtime for a variety of reasons. Sometimes students truly want to get work done, but more often they want to socialize with friends. And then there are the students who wish to escape to the library.

Adding to the challenge, schedules in the high school often mean some students are at lunch while others are in class. As a result, you are frequently working with a class during other students' lunch periods. Fortunately, your classes should have a lot of group work and research activities. Divide your time between checking on the progress of those in your class and overseeing the behavior of your lunch drop-ins.

Drop-Ins—Teachers, Administrators, and Guests

Unlike in the classroom, teachers, the principal, and other guests often drop into the library. Teachers may come to use the copy machine or the laminator or other special equipment that is kept in the library. Although it's good that they are accustomed to using the library, sometimes they take advantage of your time and ask you a questions or even schedule classes. Although you want to attend to them, your students come first. Let them know you will be with them as soon as you complete what you are doing—and do whatever must be done to ensure kids are engaged in their task.

Administrators drop by, frequently unannounced. They may be alone or have guests. If you are involved with a class, signal with your head to acknowledge their presence. Don't stop working with your class or an individual student until there is an appropriate break. Ask the administrator if there is anything you can do for them. You can briefly mention what the class is doing, and then return to your students. Do not use this time to complain about something or promote the library program.

Covering a Class

One of the most onerous duties is being asked to cover a class for a teacher. It may be for a single period or for the entire day. In the former case, the teacher may have a meeting or have to leave early for something like a doctor's appointment. In the latter situation, it may be that the teacher is out for the day and a substitute was unobtainable.

You are more likely to face this situation at the middle and high school levels, because the fixed schedule at the elementary level means teachers are deprived of their library prep period if you are covering all day. In some districts, you may be compensated if you must use your own free period to cover a class. Although this is a nice small bonus, you don't have a choice of whether or not to take a class, which disrupts what you have planned for that day.

Let your principal know of any classes you are asked to cover. Ask advice for how teachers should be informed that their scheduled library time is cancelled. This can result in the administrator making a change that allows you to keep your original schedule. Alternatively, ask if the class can meet in the library. This gives you the comfort of being in your own space. You can usually adapt the teacher's lesson plan to incorporate information skills. Make sure students are aware you will be reporting to the teacher about how the class went. Knowing they will be accountable will help to minimize the behavior students often engage in when they have a sub.

On occasion, something occurs that requires an entire class to leave their classroom. It could be anything from a chemistry experiment gone wrong to a student vomiting. The bottom line is the class must be accommodated, and the library is the first go-to location.

You are not likely to see this in elementary school because your library is probably too small to fit a second class, but middle and high school librarians do face this situation on occasion. Inform any class you are working with that another class is coming in, and that you will need to speak to the teacher once students arrive.

When your "guests" enter, let the teacher know where the class should sit. Find out if anything is needed and do your best to accommodate the teacher. How well this works depends a great deal on your relationship with the teacher and the makeup of the class. It may not go as well as you like, but hopefully the problem will be cleared up in one period.

Disruptions are a fact of life for the school librarian. You can prepare for many of them, but you will never anticipate all possible scenarios. What will help you the most is the environment you have created for your library and the relationships you have built with students and teachers.

Book Fairs

Whether you run the book fair or the parent association does, the library will be the venue. The concept is great. You want to get books into the hands of students. Ownership of books promotes reading. If you get to keep the profits, they can go toward buying more books for the library. (Note also that companies such as Scholastic give you bonus "dollars" to spend, which stretch your earnings further.)

These benefits come with a price. If you are running the book fair—and possibly even if you are not— you will be the one to contact the company and select the date. The preparation will include scheduling classes in twice, once to look and once to buy.

Be mindful of kids who look but don't buy. Chances are they don't have the money. Note what catches their eye and do what you can to give them the book. These kids are under more stress than we are aware of. Doing small things can make a big difference.

You must decide how much non-book material to allow. Toys and games tend to be preferred by kids, but this runs counter to the goal of having students own books. Work with the book fair company to keep these non-book materials to a minimum.

Volunteers are a must. They help you unpack and set up the tables, assist with sales, and, if you're lucky, help you pack up what is left to ship back to the company. If you have a volunteer you know and trust, they can complete the financial paperwork.

If possible, don't close the library down during book fair. However, that means that while you won't have your regular classes, you'll still have drop-ins. You will need to attend to them while keeping an eye on the students shopping at the book fair. Student drop-ins are likely to attempt to browse along with the class. You need to get them to complete whatever they were supposed to do and return to their class.

DEFIANCE

Beyond the many distractions and disruptions, you also need to contend with defiance. Defiance can be viewed as an extreme form of disruption. Fortunately, this is not as common as the disruptions discussed above, but it will have a greater impact on your day. Although classroom teachers also deal with defiance, the unique situation in the library classroom makes this a far greater challenge. You need to be aware of a variety of interventions to keep these incidents from escalating.

Confrontational behavior from students always makes for a tense time. Not only do you have the defiant student to deal with, you also have to pay attention to the other students in the class and the library itself. They are observing it all, and it will affect how they view and trust you.

In chapter 1, we discussed Power Over, Power Within, and Power With. Being aware of these three manifestations of power is critical in dealing with defiance. First you need to be sure you are not coming from Power Over. Ideally, you can use Power With to reach out to the student.

Recognize the student is using Power Over. You want to be able to use Power Within so they can regain control of themselves. Despite how it seems, they don't enjoy being out of control and will appreciate it if you can help them rein themselves in (although they probably will never tell you that).

Defiance is exhibited at escalating levels.

Confrontational Questions and Statements

Students may ask, "Why are we learning this again?" or "Why do we have to know this?" Their tone of voice is an immediate indication of their desire to get a rise out of you.

Response: Just because the tone was challenging, that doesn't mean it isn't a good question. Answer calmly and honestly. If it is a repeat learning experience, was it done accidentally or is there an important clarification that you can explain? Although you should know why you are teaching something (hence, essential questions), it may take a moment to come up with an answer to the second question. Be honest. You will find some advice on ways to handle this from Anna May Tempus's "When Am I Ever Going to Use This?" [2]

Anger and Hostility

An angry, hostile student is one of the most challenging disruptions. From the first, the student is loud and argumentative. In many cases they enjoy the attention from the other students—and you.

Response: Don't yell at the student. Move closer to them, but don't invade their territory. Recognize this behavior almost always has nothing to do with you. The anger may have been triggered in the previous class or the in hallway before students entered the library. Ask if they need help. This can distract them from the tirade. If that doesn't work, say something like, "You are having a tough day. I am going to get you some paper and a pen. Write down what is upsetting you. You don't have to share it. Just get it out." Will this work? If you have developed a relation with this student, it probably will. Sometimes, it doesn't work. If the anger can't be tamped down, the student could become more volatile. You might have to bring an administrator in, but that should be your last resort. Follow up on a day when the student is calm. Let them know you wish the situation hadn't gotten out of hand. This is where you can begin to build a relationship if you haven't yet developed one.

Violence

When a student's anger and frustration become too much for them to handle, they may erupt into violent behavior. They may knock over a chair or a display or even, if a personal conflict is involved, strike another student.

Response: Assess how serious the situation is. If it's violent, you need to get a security guard in. You must ensure the safety of your students and yourself. Do not be confrontational, however, if you know the student, you can move closer to them and say something like, "I know you are very upset and angry. I can help if you tell me what is wrong." It may not work. In any case, you need to inform the office.

PBISworld.com identifies thirty-six challenging behaviors ranging alphabetically from "Anxiety" to "Unable to Work Independently."[3] Clicking on any behavior opens a description of it. If a behavior applies to a student, click again for interventions suggestions.

Oppositional Defiant Disorder

The most troubling type of defiance is called Oppositional Defiant Disorder (ODD). Students who have this disorder have frequent outbursts, may use inappropriate language, and can act out physically. An article from *We Are Teachers* describes the disorder and explains some of the underlying causes and how to manage the behavior.[4] Note that if you are dealing with a student with ODD, you need to be in communication with guidance counselors and know what resources are at your disposal.

In all these situations, and the many other ones you will deal with, you must not get drawn into the student's behavior. If they get a reaction from you—yelling at them or stopping the lesson—it means you have lost charge of the situation. You are no longer managing the library environment.

Think back to the discussion on power in chapter 1. Acts of defiance and some types of disruptions are examples of students employing Power Over.

You won't win by trying to outdo them in this power confrontation. Use your Power With to de-escalate the situation.

Don't bother asking, "What were you thinking?" or "Why did you do that?" A person's cerebral cortex, the portion that deals with consequences of actions, is not fully developed until about age twenty. The student really won't know why they did it. As noted earlier, an idea comes into their head and they go with it—never thinking of what might result.

Here are some comments about challenges, disruptions, and defiance from librarians in the field.

Elementary School
"I have the hardest time when students are in conflict with one another. Tattletales, dirty looks, side remarks.... Mediation is time-consuming and I never know if I've actually handled it well."

"Usually, it's an ongoing issue from the classroom that's not going to be resolved in the library."

Handle both of these situations by having students sit apart from each other. As noted, the behavior rarely started in the library.

Middle School
"Students cannot handle the unstructured time to search for books and end up hanging out. As a result, I do not offer much time to search for materials, and therefore have a low checkout rate. I realize it's classroom management, and it's only the few who ruin it, but I struggle with how to better handle this...keeping those few engaged while I help student who want to find and read books."

"Getting students to stop talking/tapping/getting out their phones during lessons."

Handle this by putting books on display for students to choose from. Ask what their favorite genres are so you can put them out next time.

In the second case, say something like, "Finish what you are saying and then [insert whatever they should be doing]." As for phones, tell them "Put it away or I will hold it until the end of the period."

High School
"Foul language, noise, failure to follow requests, for example, 'Please follow the dress code by taking off your hat, earbuds, etc.,' disrespectful attitude which usually includes colorful language, and 'I don't have to listen to you,' 'I don't want to take this exam,' 'I don't like you anyway,' etc."

Handle by repeating what you need to say, for example, "That language is not acceptable" or "Please lower your voice." Don't respond to the student's arguments. Just keep repeating the statement.

"The biggest problem is keeping order during the lunch periods when the people in the cafeteria give passes to students to come to the media center during lunch. Then I get the disrespect, foul language, students ignoring me, or giving me a hard time when I ask them to sign in upon entering, doing flips onto the bean bag chairs... I haven't been at the school that long, don't know the (1,000+) students by name, so I don't know when they give fake names or who to report if they break rules. That's a big challenge. Teachers have a roster of who is in the room, and at lunch I do not."

But here's an encouraging comment from another librarian:

"It has gotten much better than when I started. I ask the café staff to get the names of the students who take the passes and match the names with list of students who sign in. I've had security view camera footage to ID offenders from hallway footage (there are no cameras in media center), but it's not perfect."

Lunch is a challenge. Post a sign where students sign in explaining the reason it is necessary for them to do so. You can also limit the number of passes to the library during lunch.

I hope this list of distractions and disruptions does not scare you off. This is the reality. Some of it is caused by when the physical layout of the library is too tempting for those students who feel constrained by the classroom. Some of it is caused by the school environment. At the middle and high school levels, note whether the administration enforces rules on foul language and using devices. If rules aren't enforced or the kids think are trivial, you can expect them to break them.

And some of this is caused by the librarian. As I said earlier, if the lesson isn't engaging, students will find a variety of ways to tune out, and these will lead to disruptions. Learning opportunities where students can satisfy their curiosity and pursue their interests, are able move around, and can work in small groups will help keep them focused. Although students bring attitudes from what happened in class or in the hall on the way to the library, when the behaviors stem from boredom, you need to look at yourself.

SOCIAL AND EMOTIONAL LEARNING AND TRAUMA-SENSITIVE INSTRUCTION

Social and emotional learning (SEL) has been incorporated into many school curriculums in recognition that students at all levels are stressed by difficult situations at home, by the demands of school, and by testing. It affects their learning and ultimately their ability to be successful.

The open space of the library gives students under stress a larger territory in which to let their emotions loose. Not being in their regular environment with its familiar routines and patterns can be triggers for negative behaviors. Somehow you need to make it a safe place for them.

Schools that embody SEL in their teaching draw information from the Center for Social and Emotional Learning. Its framework has five core competencies:

- Self-Awareness
- Self-Management
- Social Awareness
- Relationship Skills
- Responsible Decision-Making[5]

The explanation of how these competencies show up in school (and at home) illustrates the importance of teaching from a SEL approach. Even if your school hasn't embraced the philosophy, you can do so within the library.

Along with SEL, you'll need to develop an understanding of trauma-informed teaching. An article in *Education Week* referred to a report from the National Survey on Children's Health which stated that over 45 percent of children had suffered at least one adverse childhood experience (ACE).[6] These include experiencing or witnessing abuse, the incarceration of a parent, the death of a parent, and witnessing or being involved in a violent act outside of the home.

Students with ACE can act out unpredictably. Because you don't know the root cause, almost anything can set them off, and they go into fight—and sometimes flight—mode. It's bad enough when it happens in a class. In the library the effects are magnified.

It is no wonder students act out. There is upheaval and uncertainty in their lives. Often the adults who should be trusted caregivers are not present or are part of the problem. Under the circumstances, they may not trust you just because you are an adult. Every time you challenge them, they are likely to respond in a hostile way, even when you don't think that you were confrontational.

One simple strategy is to have students change their breathing pattern. When anyone goes into fight or flight, breathing becomes shallow and rapid. By slowing the breathing, calm is more easily restored. Rather than instructing the student to take deep breaths, join them. Say, "Let's just breathe together for a while. One breath in. Hold. One breath out. Hold." Breathe with the student. It will help calm your jittery nerves as well.

Before you can change students' behavior and keep your library a safe, welcoming environment, you may need to change your own behavior. In addition to incorporating SEL, adjust your practice so that it is trauma-informed. The theme of the October 2019 issue of *Educational Leadership* is "Making School a Safe Place." Jessica Minahan's article "Trauma-Informed Teaching Strategies" presents information on how to do that.[7]

Minahan uses the analogy of these students being like a soda can sitting on a desk. You don't know if it's been shaken. If it has, it will explode on opening. You can't stop all explosions, but you can take preventative measures to minimizes the number and intensity of the episodes.

First, as always, build relationships with students. It will take time to build relationships with those students with ACE. Trust is not the only issue when emotions are raw. Some of your innocuous questions can set off a reaction. Asking what they did last summer or on their vacation moves them emotionally from the relative safety of school to the turmoil that is their home life. Don't give orders. "Line up" sounds innocent, but it's better to give an explanation first. Let everyone know the period is coming to an end and it's time to line up. Routines, as discussed in chapter 3 are also helpful. Students need to know what is coming next.

Sharing your interests will make you a "real person." Ask students to tell you about the best book they ever read. You can let them know this is how you can find more books like it. Make a positive comment about a t-shirt.

As much as possible allow students to make decisions on acceptable behavior, just as you do with their other learning experiences. By giving students choice and voice they take ownership of their actions. Review the stages of development in chapter 1 as a reminder of what students' needs are at different ages.

RESTORATIVE JUSTICE

Historically, students who engaged in highly disruptive or defiant behaviors were punished, usually with suspension. That temporarily eliminated the problem, but the student's behavior didn't change when they returned to school. Repeated suspensions frequently led to them dropping out of school, which negatively affected their futures.

In an effort to turn the situation around, schools have been turning to restorative justice. Using mediation and agreement, this approach seeks to have the offender make amends in some way and accept responsibility along with a plan to change behavior. By involving the offender in the process, makes them a part of the solution.

An article from *We Are Teachers* compares restorative justice with traditional approaches.[8] It summarizes the three tiers that form the path: prevention, intervention, and reintegration. The article presents seven questions that help illustrate how this approach differs from other disciplinary methods.

Restorative justice is not simple. It takes time and effort to put it into practice. During your career in education, it's likely you have become well aware that all too often educators, including librarians, are not given the training needed when a new approach is introduced. For a school to use the model successfully, everyone needs to understand their role and what behaviors to employ.

If your school does not use restorative justice to deal with negative behaviors, consider how you can employ it within the library. The seven questions in the *We Are Teachers* article are a good start to help you address such behavior and keep it from escalating. Once you have gained some experience, speak with administrators about how it might be implemented schoolwide.

FINAL THOUGHTS

For more help, see Katrina Schwartz's "Twenty Tips to De-Escalate Interactions with Anxious or Defiant Students."[9] The more you learn about the root cause of negative behaviors the easier it will be to prevent or defuse it. You will never eliminate all incidents, but you will not be thrown off balance when they occur.

By treating all students with respect, you show that you care about them. In doing so, you create a climate that minimizes confrontations. And when a problem occurs, you will be as prepared as you can be to handle it.

KEY IDEAS

- Distractions and disruptions occur in all classrooms, but their effects are magnified within the library classroom.
- Outside circumstances, students, teachers, and others contribute to distractions and disruptions in the library.
- Defiance is the most extreme form of disruptions you will face.
- Although classroom teachers contend with defiance, this behavior is sometimes exacerbated in the unique environment of the library.
- Because students don't see the librarian as their teacher, their behavior and responses are more difficult to manage than in the classroom.
- Prevention and preparation help you to respond effectively to distractions and disruptions.
- Student disruptions include talking, horseplay, and zoning out. Each can be managed with an appropriate intervention.
- Events like fire drills and lockdowns create havoc with your lesson. Know the protocols and have your class roster and sign-in sheets at hand.
- Student drop-ins need to be monitored even as you are simultaneously teaching a class.

- As soon as the students you are teaching are working, check in with a drop-in to ensure that the person has signed in and knows what they are to do.
- Even during the best lessons, there will be students who disrupt the class.
- Being prepared for these disruptions and remaining calm are the first steps in restoring order.
- Have several strategies for dealing with the disruptive student with a minimum of fuss.
- Know in advance how you will respond if you are told to substitute for a teacher.
- When teachers and administrators drop in, deal with your class or individual student before turning to help them.
- Book fairs are great way to get students excited about reading.
- Work with the book fair company to keep non-book items to a minimum.
- Decide whether the library will be open during book fairs.
- Defiance is an extreme form of disturbance, and you need to know how to deal with its different forms.
- Defiant students may be angry, hostile or even violent.
- Knowing how to respond and understanding underlying causes can keep these episodes to a minimum.
- Come from Power With when dealing with defiant students and recognize they are using Power Over.
- Defiant behavior is exhibited at different levels of hostility. React accordingly.
- Real-life examples of disruptive and defiant behavior reveal the stress they cause and provide ways of dealing with these incidents.
- Students who have had adverse childhood experiences are living with trauma that can erupt into defiant behaviors.
- Social and emotional learning and trauma-informed teaching can help these students and reduce the number of incidents.
- In restorative justice, the offender takes responsibility and compensates for any resulting damage. This positive method leads to fewer suspensions and helps students learn how to improve their behavior.

NOTES

1. Linda Shalaway, "Twenty-Five Sure-Fire Strategies for Handling Difficult Students," *Teachers,* Scholastic.com, 2005, https://www.scholastic.com/teachers/articles/teaching-content/25-sure-fire-strategies-handling-difficult-students/.
2. Anna May Tempus, "When Am I Ever Going to Use This?" *Edutopia,* January 21, 2019, https://edut.to/2Vpyka 5.

3. "Welcome to PBIS World! Click on a Behavior to Start," PBIS World, https://www .pbisworld.com/.

4. "What Teachers Need to Know About Students with ODD (Oppositional Defiant Disorder)," *We Are Teachers,* April 2, 2019, https://www.weareteachers.com/ students-with-odd/?utm_content=1576266888&utm_medium=social&utm _source=facebook&fbclid=IwAR3-wzix3Hfjl044YGAi1twbQKDweHvj4AlQz9TkG vORBEG8qoQN4QMKSrk.

5. Collaborative for Academic, Social, and Emotional Learning, "Core SEL Competencies," https://casel.org/core-competencies/.

6. "Student Trauma Is Widespread: Schools Don't Have to Go It Alone," *Education Week,* February 26, 2018, https://www.edweek.org/ew/articles/2018/02/26/ student-trauma-is-widespread-schools-dont-have-to-go-alone.html.

7. Jessica Minahan, "Trauma-Informed Teaching Strategies," *Educational Leadership* 77, no.2 (October 2019), 30–35.

8. "What Teachers Need to Know About Restorative Justice," *We Are Teachers,* January 15, 2019, https://www.weareteachers.com/restorative-justice/.

9. Katrina Schwartz, "Twenty Tips to De-Escalate Interactions with Anxious or Defiant Students," KQED, January 15, 2019, https://www.kqed.org/ mindshift/43049/20-tips-to-help-de-escalate-interactions-with-anxious-or -defiant-students.

7

Time Management, Clubs, and Other Uses of the Library

B y this time, you recognize that as a school librarian you are constantly juggling many balls. It seems overwhelming, and it can be. Even experienced librarians are harried. There are just not enough hours in the day.

Along with your teaching, you have likely taken on responsibility for STEAM, the makerspace, or coding. Add to these activities such as book clubs and extracurricular clubs. And you still have a library to run. Most of you don't have clerical help, and even if you do, behind-the-scenes library work takes time. Time management becomes a survival skill.

TIME MANAGEMENT

Just about all of us could use a few more hours in the day. Unless you develop support strategies you'll end almost every day and week exhausted. If you don't do something about it, you will eventually burn out. Much of our exhaustion comes from doing tasks that don't connect with the bigger picture. With a mission and a vision for your library program, you can better see the ultimate purpose of even small tasks and quickly notice if you are furthering your mission or being pulled away from it.

A quick search of the internet reveals numerous articles on time management. Most of the advice is repeated in some way. Although they all have elements that apply to what you do, they don't take into account the unique challenge of managing the school library classroom.

Barbara Bond's blog post "Too Much to Do, Too Little Time? Time Management Helps" has suggestions that make sense in our world.[1] One of her most helpful points is knowing which tasks require concentrated time and which can be done more quickly. If you take on a more complicated task when you only have a few minutes to work, the interruptions will cause you to lose concentration, you will work harder, and accomplish less.

A to-do list is a classic way to manage time, but just noting down tasks is not enough and a long list can be overwhelming to look at. And if it's overwhelming, you're likely not to check it and will end up missing something. Consider putting a star by high-priority tasks, then look at your schedule and decide when during your day these priority tasks can be done.

Use spare minutes to clear non-urgent tasks such as reading e-mail, opening snail mail, or looking at social media. These are also good to do at the end of the day when you are tired and are not in a place to be creative.

We all know that part of our challenge is the time that gets wasted. It's important to note that there's a difference between procrastinating and preparing to switch gears. The brain requires a pause before shifting from one activity to another. You need to do something mindless after being creative before moving to another demanding task. You might play another game (or ten) of Klondike before you move on to your next task.

Note what you are working on and what you are avoiding when you procrastinate. Identify which of the tasks you ignore are caused by your brain telling you it needs a pause and which tasks you are dodging. Be honest with yourself as to why you are putting something off and then find a way to tackle it. For most people, working on it the first thing in the morning is effective, even if it's necessary to come in early to do so. It's amazing how free you will feel once it's completed.

Discover the most efficient way for you to move from one task to another. But also allow yourself to do something like play Klondike—or whatever game you choose—every now and then. You do need a break.

As you can imagine, there are many business-oriented articles concerned with maximizing available time. "A List of Suggestions to Become More Productive," by Naphtali Hoff offers ideas.[2] All thirteen (presented below in random order) begin with the letter "S."

1. *Stop.* Before plunging into the next task, reflect on what you want to achieve. As I would phrase it, "What will best further my mission?"
2. *Set goals.* As Yogi Berra said, "If you don't know where you are going, you will wind up someplace else." Goals remind you of what you want to achieve.

3. *Segment and celebrate.* Small, short-term goals are best. Each time you accomplish one, it gives you a boost to the next one. Break down large jobs into small, attainable goals. Give yourself small rewards when you reach a goal. (Perhaps one game of Klondike.)
4. *Simplify.* What can be done to make the task less complex? Identifying short-term goals will help.
5. *[Get] Serious.* Let someone know about your goal. We are more likely to hold ourselves accountable if we have a partner who is aware of what we did or didn't do.
6. *Schedule, schedule, schedule.* Hoff is not a fan of to-do lists, but he recommends blocking out time for tasks, which is similar to my suggestion to consider jobs according to how long they are likely to take.
7. *Strategize.* This is related to scheduling. What is the best time for each task? Most people are more creative in the mornings. This is not the time for simpler tasks such as e-mail.
8. *Snooze (your devices).* Set a time to focus on e-mail, which also means not checking it while you are in the middle of another job that requires your full attention.
9. *Smile.* It creates a positive atmosphere, not only with others—it also affects your posture and demeanor.
10. *Stretch.* As a walker, I know the benefits of stepping away from the computer and doing something physical. It doesn't need to take long, but it needs doing. It's been said that sitting is the new cigarette smoking.
11. *Snack.* Eat something healthy like fruit, vegetable sticks, or a small yogurt. It will power you back up. Do not indulge in junk food.
12. *Sleep.* Trying to get more done by cutting down on sleep doesn't work. Your brain will fog, you will become less productive, and you'll make errors.
13. *Self-care.* Not taking care of yourself, which includes not getting enough sleep, is debilitating. You stop giving your best. Your job is not your first priority (or it shouldn't be). Stop behaving as though it is.

A time-management tip often given is to delegate. (Hoff probably didn't include it because it starts with a "D.") Unless you have volunteers or are lucky enough to have the very rare clerk, you don't have anyone to whom you can delegate. What you do have are colleagues. When you have built relationships with teachers, you can ask for help, which sometimes brings unexpected rewards.

I was once weeding books in the 600s. I knew many of the titles related to crafting with wood and metal were old, but this subject was beyond my personal expertise. I asked a shop teacher (we had them then) to check the books I had pulled. He was appalled by pictures of students working without safety goggles, but he also was surprised to see books in his field on my shelves. As a result of his help, he brought his class into the library for a research project.

Even experienced librarians have trouble prioritizing tasks. Teaching a scheduled class obviously takes precedence over everything else. The difficulty lies in determining the importance of other demands of the job.

For example, getting books back on the shelf is important. It's been estimated that it takes about two minutes per book to process a return and put it back to its place on the shelf. Is it a priority? Yes, but it's not more important than setting up for the next class.

Consider how to handle it differently. You can leave the books in order on the cart, prepared for shelving, but not keep the cart tucked close to the desk. Instead, you can put a sign on the cart saying, "Just returned. Are you interested?" Any books that are checked out save you shelving time.

Many of you will have limited budgets and don't do much book ordering, but it does take time to get the books from the carton and onto the shelves. Is it a priority? To a degree, but not as much as you might think.

Checking off the new arrivals is a higher priority, because you need to inform the accounts payable secretary that the books have arrived so the vendor can be paid. If you have volunteers, they can handle that. They can also do the property stamping and other clerical tasks needed to identify it as the library's book.

But the books shouldn't be shelved until you have checked the Dewey number (or the genre code) in case you need to make changes. These must be added not only to the spine label but also to the records (although you'll generally get the records to add to your automated system from the vendor). Important as this is, and eager as you are to put the latest additions out for student use, it's not a top priority. You can leave the books on the cart, marked "awaiting addition to the OPAC." If kids or teachers want to borrow one, you have two choices. Either reserve the title by inserting a hand-written note in the book and add the book quickly to your catalog or let them have it by signing it out specially. You can use a Google Doc for these special loans.

Time Management in Multiple Schools

Librarians who serve two or more schools face even greater time-management challenges. Chapter 4 discussed dealing with this situation in the context of collaboration with teachers and principals. Beyond making yourself known as a valued contributor, you must find a way to juggle a complex schedule.

Most likely you will have a fixed schedule as working in multiple schools occurs mostly at the elementary level. This isn't uncommon for middle school, but it's rare to be responsible for two high school libraries. Although a fixed schedule is not generally ideal, when you have multiple schools it aids in planning.

If you do work at middle or high schools and have a flexible schedule, you need a plan to reach teachers and build relationships. Start with the English or History teachers as they are most likely to work with you. Review the curriculum, and, if possible, the pacing guide so you know what is going to be taught when.

At first just e-mail teachers some relevant websites or apps along with an offer to work with the class on it. You want to do this is in small steps so that you won't be overwhelmed. As you build relationships you may also create teachers who will advocate to have you in the building more often. Although it may not happen, it's a good vision to hold

To manage the demands off multiple schools without driving yourself crazy, handle your schedule with a technique that works for large projects. I call it "telescoping, microscoping, and periscoping." It allows you to focus on the tasks at hand without losing track of the larger picture.

For the telescoping piece, start with what you will be working for the next month. Once you are comfortable with this approach, you can take a longer view. Identify what you will be teaching in each of the schools and on what day you will be doing it. What other tasks need to be accomplished in those locations? When will you do these? Are there any resources you may need that are not available in one of the schools? Where will you get them and when?

Microscoping is preparing for the next day's lesson using what you have identified during telescoping. Instead of worrying about all you have to do, only focus on the immediate need. This reduces anxiety and stress.

Because some lessons need advance preparation, use periscoping. This entails popping up to check on your telescope plan. What is coming up? Is there anything that needs your attention now or soon? By doing this, you prevent needing to scramble in the last minute to get something done. Snow days and other disruption in the schedule will require you to revise the schedule you set up when telescoping, as is true for all teachers.

As you plan your first month, look for any open blocks you can use for tasks other than teaching. Too often you are solidly booked, giving you no time for shelving, handling overdues, and the myriad of other tasks both professional and clerical. Technically, if you are working a full day in one building, you should get a free period, but this might not happen. If you find yourself in this situation, schedule a meeting with the principal or principals who set up the schedules.

Frame the meeting as a request for advice. You don't want to appear negative or whiney to a principal. Note that without any non-teaching blocks you don't know when you will be able to curate books for a class or do clerical tasks such as shelving. Have a list of what you need to do to meet student and teacher needs. Offer your suggestion to alleviate the problem and ask if they have an alternative.

The multiple-school situation becomes more of a challenge when you are split between two schools on the same day. Do your best to get this changed. Point out that the schools are losing valuable library time when you are in transit.

Those assigned to three or more schools must be diligent in speaking with all the principals. Share what you hope to achieve. Acknowledge that none of you consider the situation to be ideal, but you want to make it work as best as you can for the students and teachers. Have suggestions for improvement and ask for their advice on how to proceed.

Becoming Overwhelmed

Even with the best time-management techniques, there will be times when you become overwhelmed. It's exhausting, draining, and reduces your effectiveness. It also causes short tempers and feelings of inadequacy.

You know the effects of overwhelm. You probably have read several articles on the dangers as well as how to deal with them. But while you are in it, you have no time to put any suggestions into practice. It's a Catch-22 situation.

To get to the point where you can implement strategies for dealing with overwhelm, there is one simple remedy. And you do need simple at this point. Breathe. That's it. Go to a place in your library where you won't be disturbed. Or go to the restroom. Close your eyes. Take a deep breath in and let it out. Take another and another. When you are tense and overwhelmed, your breathing becomes shallow and adds to the sensation of being out of control.

Once you have made this method your first response to feeling overwhelmed, you can employ special breathing techniques such as "square breathing." Breathe in for four seconds. Hold for four seconds. Breathe out for four seconds. Hold for four seconds. The effects are immediate.

Now that you have a tool to deal with those moments, you need a plan to minimize the frequency of attacks. When you live in an almost constant state of overwhelm, your logical thinking is affected, you don't bring your best to your family and friends (actually, you probably bring your worst), and your attitude sends negative signals to teachers and students.

Our world runs 24/7. Information, questions, and problems keep coming in, and you feel duty-bound to respond—sometimes immediately. That gives you little time to think and set priorities. You become more overwhelmed.

Time out. Breathe. You are not alone. Those of us in education are not the only ones dealing with overwhelm. The business world recognizes this problem as well. The *Harvard Business Review* website offers a post from Rebecca Zucker titled "How to Deal with Constantly Feeling Overwhelmed."[3] She offers five suggestion. (But breathe first!)

- ***Pinpoint the primary source of overwhelm.*** You may give everything equal weight, but that's not reality. Some things stress you more. Is it a project? An aspect of your schedule? A personal issue? You probably can't take it off your plate, but by identifying it, you can analyze why it is weighing so heavily on you, and what can be done to reduce the stress somewhat. For example, if it's a project, break it down into pieces so you don't feel the weight of the entire thing all at once.

- *Set boundaries on your time and workload.* This is hard for some of you. You can't work late every day and spend your weekend hours doing more work for school. For those of you who are workaholics, give yourself at least two days when you leave early and one day free on the weekend. You will have more energy and do better work in a shorter amount of time. This is one of those cases when less is more.

- *Challenge your perfectionism.* Not everything needs to be completed to the same degree of perfection, whether it's a display or end-of-day cleanup. It you are working at two or more schools, stop trying do full-time work in all your schools. Discuss priorities with your administrators to let them know what you think is most important and what you cannot do because of your schedule. Ask them for their advice and work with it. (This also relates to setting boundaries on your workload.)

- *Outsource or delegate.* This is a tough one. Can you get student volunteers? They may be more work at the beginning, but they can help. Can you incorporate some task into your lessons? At the elementary level, kids can learn to put returned books on the cart in shelf order. Little things help. On the home front, perhaps you can hire someone to clean or do yard work so that you have more free time during the weekend .

- *Challenge your assumptions.* What would happen if you didn't do one of your jobs? I used to be upset about processing new books and racing to get them on the shelves. Instead, I decided to let teachers and students see them. If they wanted one, they could borrow it, I would make a note of it, and process it when it was returned. It got material out faster and was a lure to be the first to read it.

- *Start putting these suggestions into practice.* Note how many require a change of thinking. And yes, there will still be days when you feel overwhelmed. Just breathe.

Just remember, some days none of this works. Life happens. Accept it. Tomorrow is another day.

STEAM

Those who do not work in education still think of the library as "the book place." They mentally store it with English language arts. (My supervisors at the high school level have been in charge of that subject area and social stud-ies.) People see those areas as natural for research, which they are, but don't see the library doing anything for other subjects.

That view was always limiting and is even more so now. In today's world, activities included under the umbrella of school libraries keep expanding. Makerspaces that incorporate STEAM (science, technology, engineering, art, and mathematics) have found a home in many school libraries, as have coding and Genius Hour. The latter was intended for classrooms, but librarians have embraced it because having students explore their passions and develop their creativity seem a natural fit for the library program.

Developing, maintaining, and expanding these new functions have added to librarian's responsibilities. Although some districts have made these the centerpiece of the library, sometimes to the extent of eliminating books, these activities do have an important place.

One of the four Domains in the *National School Library Standards* is Cre-ate, which is central to these activities. In a well-designed makerspace, stu-dents learn as they create through the Shared Foundations, such as Inquire, Collaborate, and Explore. As the librarian, you will also curate print and digital resources for students to use.

If you are just beginning a makerspace, draw on the experiences of other librarians. There are books and countless articles online that will help. Look for those geared to your grade level plan to start small. You need to see how it fits into your day so that you're not overwhelmed. Your planning should also include ways for the makerspace to grow and evolve. Student interest is your guide to where to take it next. They can be a great source of help.

Students can become teachers by sharing their expertise. High school stu-dents from the robotics club can help at elementary and middle schools. If you have a makerspace evening, parents, and possibly local business people, can lead the activity. This is a good community outreach that serves as advocacy for the library program.

Coding is a part of many library programs now. You can begin through Hour of Code (https://hourofcode.com/us). Again, don't launch this program without getting advice from other librarians. This is where your personal learning network (PLN) will help.

As noted, although Genius Hour is often done in the classroom, it has a natural place in the library. Addie Matteson's article in *School Library Journal* explains what a Genius Hour is and how to fit it into your program. It is more challenging than a makerspace or coding, but it has proved successful.[4]

LEGO clubs and board games can entice students who don't usually choose to go to the library. It's another way to show the library is a safe, wel-coming environment for all.

Important as it is, the library is not just about STEAM. At its core it is about books and the love of reading. Connect these activities to your collec-tion. Have fiction and nonfiction on display that reinforces and stimulates thinking to expand on what students produce. Remember your mission and be sure you are furthering it within these programs.

As you add these new features, administrators may start to think that the library is no longer about books and that books aren't necessary. From there it's one step to deciding the librarian is not necessary because a tech specialist can run these activities. You need to make the library uniquely yours.

Other Activities

The library program is about more than a curriculum and lesson plans. Its programs are yours to design. They should meet the needs of all your teachers and students. To do so requires you to be alert for more ways to involve and engage stakeholders.

Book Clubs

Librarians are increasingly incorporating book clubs into their program to foster a love of reading and create a culture of literacy. Book clubs make reading a social experience. In some places, they are held during lunch. The kids get to eat their lunch and discuss books. Some clubs have a theme, others don't. You might focus on one topic for a few months, then try a different topic. See what students want.

A somewhat more unusual book club is one for adults and children. A two-week time frame can work for this. The student chooses a book and a parent or guardian also reads it. They discuss it as they continue to read at home. At the end of the two weeks have all participants meet in the library and talk about the books they read. It is fascinating to see the differences in what the student got from the book and what the adult did. This kind of club was led by a teacher in a school where I was the librarian. I remember a mother-son pair who read Hank Aaron's book *I Had a Hammer*. The son couldn't understand why Aaron was persecuted. The discussion at home was so lively that the father decided to read the book as well. In all cases, a stronger bond between parent and child developed, and the love of reading increased.

"One Book, One School" programs have proved very popular. Do some research before launching this month-long activity. Sam Northern's *Knowledge Quest* blog post, "One School + One Book = A Love of Reading," is an excellent introduction and overview.[5] Use your PLN for advice about choosing the right book. Make sure you can obtain enough copies. The public library may be able to help.

Sell the idea to students by designing an introduction to capture their interest. (You'll find many suggestions online.) Next work on getting as many adults involved as you can. The more people in your building who are part of it the better. Reach out to the parents as well. Have some sort of closing celebration that acknowledges the joys of reading together.

Book Fairs Redux

Chapter 6 looked at book fairs as one of the distractions that occur in the library, but there are other aspects to consider. They are most common at the elementary level. Classes come at their regular library times. Book fairs are a great way to get kids excited about books. As noted in the that chapter, they can also serve as a fund-raiser for the library.

Some librarians love book fairs. Others dread them. For many it's a mix of the two. Knowing how rewarding it is for kids to own books and seeing their obvious pleasure when buying the books they want is a reward for all our efforts to nurture their love of books. At the same time, book fairs are exhausting. The preparation before, the constant parade of student and sometimes parents during the fair, the accounting, boxing up, and ordering titles are draining. Where you stand depends on how much help you have, how much of the profits you keep, and how well your vendor works with you.

If you have never held a book fair, ask members of your PLN about recommendations for vendors. Some use local bookstores; others prefer larger providers such as Scholastic or Follett. After you have run the first fair in your school, assess the experience. Did the vendor do what you expected? Was the follow-up good? How open were they to hear from you? You can always change vendors the next year.

Take an active role in dealing with the fair vendor. They often send non-book items including pencils to games. Avoid these so that kids don't spend their money on these items rather than books.

Be alert for students who don't have money to buy books. Have some titles prepared to give them in a quiet way. You don't want them to feel left out. It's part of how you make the library safe for them, too.

Author Visits

Author visits require classroom management skills. The visits contribute to kids' excitement about books and reading. Visits usually cost a fair amount of money which, hopefully the parent organization will fund. Some authors are willing to Skype for free or a lower fee. Because author visits can be difficult to arrange, you may want to wait until you have been in your school for at least a year.

Use your PLN to help find authors who communicate well with kids. Spend several months preparing students for the visit. Read different books by the author or illustrator. Discuss their common themes and how they may differ.

Guide students into developing good questions to ask. You don't want them just asking, "How much money do you make?" Have the kids (possibly with the help of the art teacher) decorate the library and/or the halls in a way to welcome the author.

Co- and Extracurricular Activities

Despite your very full days, you must make time to ensure you are a visible presence in your school. Otherwise you run the risk of being eliminated when budgets tighten, as they regularly do. One way to become known "outside" the library is to take on a co- or extracurricular activity.

At the middle and high school levels, look for clubs that have natural connections to the library or to your personal interests. I was the advisor for the Academic Decathlon team in one school. Winning championships and bringing home trophies put my students—and me—in the limelight.

One middle school librarian started a literary magazine. Another worked on the yearbook. Include these activities on your library webpage. It is good outreach to parents and demonstrates your value to administrators. At first, they may not see the "library part," but as the relationship develops over your activity, they will.

At all levels, serving on school and district committees can enhance your reputation. You bring a unique perspective that others will appreciate (particularly it you know how to express it well). Choose from those committees that are likely to have an impact on the school or district.

The welcoming atmosphere—and size—of the library make it the natural location for a variety of school activities. Everything from faculty meetings, parent organization meetings, and parties for the faculty are held in the library. On a professional development day, refreshments are often served in the library. Honor society and other club inductions usually meet in the library, and, in some places, the board of education might meet there.

Depending on which group is using the library and for what purpose you may or may not be in attendance. When you can be there, it's a good idea to do so. In any case, you need to clean up the library in advance. Make sure your desk is neat, even if you must stuff things in a file cabinet. The library sends a message. You know that a too-neat library during the school year means that it's not being used, but that's not how visitors will see it. Cleaning up is extra work, but it will avoid any negative impressions people might develop about the library.

🔲 KEY IDEAS

- To accomplish your many tasks and roles, you need to become skilled at time management.
- Identify which tasks are urgent and which can wait. (Your mission can be a guide.)
- Work on tasks appropriate to the amount of time you have available during the best time of day for you to deal with them.
- You'll feel overwhelmed. When you do, remember to breathe.

- Have a go-to strategy to deal with overwhelm.
- If you have a flex schedule with middle and high schools, learn the English and History curriculums and send teachers relevant websites and apps to build relationships and collaboration.
- Use telescoping, microscoping, and periscoping to time-manage multiple schools.
- Meet with the principals in the schools you serve to find solutions for the challenges caused by your time being divided between two or more buildings.
- STEAM and STEAM-related activities have found a place in school library programs.
- Connect activities to books to ensure that your unique role in the program is seen and valued.
- Lunchtime book clubs centering on a theme attract readers. Rotate among a variety of topics to reach more students and keep interest alive.
- "One Book, One School" programs bring in a broad range of stakeholders, stimulate discussions about reading, and showcase the library program.
- Planning a book fair takes time. After the book fair, asses the vendor to see if you need to make a change.
- Have books available for those kids who don't have money to buy any.
- Author visits are time-consuming and expensive, but very valuable.
- Work with teachers to prepare students for an author visit, including writing meaningful questions.
- Consider getting involved in a co– or extracurricular activity so you'll become known outside of the library.
- Membership on a school or district committee is a good way to show your particular expertise.

NOTES

1. Barbara Bond, "Too Much to Do, Too Little Time? Time Management Helps," November 8, 2016, http://barbara567band.blogspot.com/2016/11/too-much -to-do-too-little-time-time.html.
2. Naphtali Hoff, "A List of Suggestions to Become More Productive," *SmartBrief*, October 10, 2018, https://bit.ly/33NdsMU.
3. Rebecca Zucker, "How to Deal with Constantly Feeling Overwhelmed," October 10, 2019, https://hbr.org/2019/10/how-to-deal-with-constantly -feeling-overwhelmed.
4. Addie Matteson, "It's Genius Hour," *School Library Journal*, October 20, 2016, https://www.slj.com/?detailStory=its-genius-hour.
5. Sam Northern, "One School + One Book = A Love of Reading," *Knowledge Quest* (blog), March 25, 2019, https://knowledgequest.aasl.org/one-school-one -book-a-love-of-reading/.

8

A Safe, Welcoming Space

For learning to succeed, students need to feel safe. Equally important, they need to feel welcome. The way you have arranged your facility, the furniture, the displays, and how you greet students show them the library welcomes them. When people who have talked about how the library was their safe haven when they were in school, they are referring to much more than the atmosphere

Making students feel welcome is important, but to truly make all students feel safe and as if they truly belong requires a more concentrated effort. Your collection needs to reflect diversity of the cultures, ethnicity, and race of your students as well as the various lifestyles they lead. Even if your school is culturally homogenous, it is necessary to show students what the larger world looks like. And while your students may look alike, there are differences that may not be apparent. These, too, must be addressed.

Socioeconomic differences and physical disabilities should be acknowledged in your collection. You need to pay attention to how students access information, making it as barrier-free as possible. To create a safe environment, you must be sensitive to the needs of those students who are "other" in some ways and work to make them feel valued and welcome.

EQUITY, DIVERSITY, AND INCLUSION

The United States is a nation of immigrants, beginning with the arrival of the first colonists and continuing to the present day. Historically, newcomers have often been looked on with suspicion and faced prejudice in different forms.

According to the U.S. Census, non-Hispanic Whites and Latinos comprise 60.7 percent of the total population of the United States.[1] That figure keeps dropping. Eventually Whites will be a minority. There are those who are openly fearful and antagonistic to this future; this may exacerbate prejudice, which too often leads to harassment, bullying, and intimidation—including physical intimidation.

It is against this backdrop that librarians must develop collection policies that address equity, diversity, and inclusion (EDI). Although the three terms may seem similar, they encompass important differences. Understanding the distinctions helps you be more attuned to your students' needs.

Equity is often confused with *equality*. An example of equality would be giving all students a Chromebook for their schoolwork, and all would have identical computers. Equity would require ensuring that all students have an equal opportunity by addressing these questions: If a computer is needed for homework, do all students have access to one at home? Can they access the internet?

You may be familiar with an illustration that is often used to explain the distinction. Three boys of different heights are trying to watch a baseball game from outside a solid fence. Equality shows them now standing on boxes of the same height. The tallest boy has an excellent view. The next one can just see over the fence. The shortest one still cannot see the game. Equity gives the boys boxes of different heights, so they all have a good view. A third panel shows the boys viewing the game from behind a chain link fence. This takes access to a more welcoming level by completely removing the barrier for all.

Diversity is a word that is frequently used to refer to various ethnicities, religions, and cultures, but it encompasses far more. Gender, gender identification, socioeconomic status are facets of diversity. So are physical and emotional challenges. Because diversity is all-encompassing it may be hard to wrap your arms around all the differences. Adding to the challenge is that so many of these differences aren't observable, certainly not on the surface. Despite that, you must work to meet the needs of all these students.

Inclusion means that everyone is a part of the whole. It would mean keeping students in age-appropriate classes. Students are not judged to be inferior because of their race, ethnicity, or physical challenges.

Consider physical disabilities. Schools do not always provide the best solutions for dealing with disabled students. The Americans with Disabilities Act of 1990 (ADA) was enacted to ensure that people with disabilities were afforded equal access as others.[2] It requires public places, including schools, to make necessary accommodations.

Although schools have made changes to comply with the law, they don't always do the best job possible. Your circulation desk should be low enough to be wheelchair accessible. Your collection must have resources suitable for those with visual challenges. (For example, you can get help from your state library's Braille and Talking Book centers.) Ask the guidance department what other disabilities students have and find solutions to meet their needs. A *Knowledge Quest* blog post shared how a school library was revamped at a special needs school.[3] Although this effort was for the whole school, it offers ideas to make your special needs students feel more welcome.

Include is the second of the six Shared Foundations in AASL's *National School Library Standards for Learners, School Librarians, and School Libraries*. The Key Commitment is "demonstrates an understanding of and commitment to inclusiveness in the learning community." The school librarian is charged with guiding learners to develop a "balanced perspective," and "empathy and tolerance for diverse ideas."[4]

Curate is the fourth Shared Foundation. It is also necessary for a diverse collection. The Key Commitment is "make meaning for oneself and others by collecting, organizing, and sharing resources of personal relevance."[5] In order for students to be able to develop a balanced perspective and global awareness, the school librarian must build a collection that will support their research.

A popular Facebook meme captured the distinction among the three terms in this way: "Accessibility is being able to get in the building. Diversity is having a seat at the table. Inclusion is having a voice at the table. Belonging is having your voice heard at the table!"

The ALA page on equity, diversity, and inclusion has numerous links to resources. The ones from ALSC and YALSA are most relevant.[6] Additionally, an interpretation of the Library Bill of Rights on Diverse Collections states: "Library workers have an obligation to select, maintain, and support access to content on subjects by diverse authors and creators that meets—as closely as possible—the needs, interests, and abilities of all the people the library serves."[7]

Although EDI is the acronym used most of the time to describe what we are trying to achieve, a better visualization is the metaphor Mirrors, Windows, and Sliding Glass Doors, as coined in an essay by Rudine Sims Bishop.[8] Students should see their lives within the library collection. *Mirrors* are the stories that show students they are visible in books and other library resources. However, Bishop notes that if children only see themselves, they develop an exaggerated sense of self-importance. *Windows* gives kids a view into a world different from their own. And *sliding glass doors* allow students to go beyond seeing other people and their lifestyle. It has them step into that world and walk in other people's shoes. This makes them tolerant and understanding of that world. You might think your collection does have mirrors but look at whether it's limited to focusing on the four "F's": food, fashion, festivals, and folklore. Although these do contribute to an understanding of differences among people, books about White people include a broader picture. By not having materials that represent their everyday lives, students still don't have a real mirror.

Jamie Campbell Naidoo states:

> As our nation continues to diversify, it is essential that children learn to understand the important role of their culture and the cultures of other people in creating an overall global culture respectful of differences. By including diversity in its programs and collections, the library has the potential for helping children make cross-cultural connections and develop the skills necessary to function in a culturally pluralistic society.[9]

He goes into detail on how to bring diversity into your program and observes that students need to see themselves in books or will feel their heritage and their very selves are not seen or valued. The student disappears. By providing mirrors for these students, you make the library a safe place.

We need to recognize that our thinking has been conditioned by our own cultural backgrounds. Naidoo's white paper does an excellent job of raising understanding about how some of these have affected our best-intentioned programs. We have also had to deal with the growing awareness of prejudice and stereotyping in some of the classics of children's and young adult literature.

Building a diverse collection is not without challenges. According to a blog post by the Cooperative Children's Book Center, the statistics on the number of books about African Americans are depressing. In 1985 when they began tracking it, out of 2,500 published books, eighteen featured African Americans. Increases were seen for a while and then leveled off in the 1990s. A few years ago, the numbers began increasing again. In 2016 it rose to 278. Although an improvement, this is certainly not a cause for celebration. The proportion is still small. Even worse, of the 278 books only 71 were written by African Americans.[10]

To further appreciate the depth of this, consider that, a high percentage of these books concern slavery or civil rights. Such books present historic issues that involved Black people, but do not portray them as people. Although Ezra Jack Keats was White, his book *A Snowy Day* (1963) was a landmark because it tells the story of the fun Peter has on a snowy day but never mentions Peter is African American. The illustrations show you that. In other words, Peter is treated as a kid. His race has nothing to do with the story.

The same situation exists for other ethnic groups. There are many stories about the holiday celebrations of different cultures. Again, as Naidoo notes, there is nothing inherently wrong in that. But if this is the only way the different groups are portrayed, there is no true picture of who they are. And students of that group don't see themselves in the library.

To make your library welcoming to all, your collection must give these students mirrors—just like White students have. Books about diverse ethnicities are also important for White students. They need windows to see into lives of people who are not exactly like them but show similar feelings and situations.

Diversity becomes an ever-expanding concept as we learn to view the world more broadly. Individual family situations are very different. You will have students with a single parent, some who have a parent serving overseas, and others who are homeless. You may have students with an incarcerated parent or sibling. You also need books that show families with two parents of the same gender. Although this can be challenging for librarians in some communities, these children need to see themselves in the library.

When students can read widely about different people, the books become sliding glass doors. They allow readers to walk in the shoes of others. As they do so, they develop tolerance. Respecting diversity and embracing differences are integral to becoming a global citizen.

LGBTQ+

LGBTQ+ kids are most likely to be bullied at school, be absent, and even commit suicide. It is imperative that these students are made to feel safe at school and in the library.

In "Rethinking Conventions: Keeping Gender-Diverse Students Safe," Anthony Ciuffo talks about kindergarteners who already wanted to dress as another gender with which they identified.[11] Ciuffo recommends building gender literacy by becoming familiar with the gender spectrum. Language also needs to change. You don't say "boys and girls" when addressing the class, and you certainly don't refer to a "boy's book" or a "girl's book."

Find out how students want to be addressed. Just as you learned how to pronounce their names or use their nickname, you need to know what pronouns they prefer. It may not be easy if we cling to outmoded conventions, but these changes are part of how we make these students feel safe.

Young adult, middle grade, and even a few picture books now portray LGBTQ+ kids. Several states now require it in the curriculum. The statistics show how much these students need mirrors, windows, and sliding glass doors. Having these books in your collection shows them they are not alone. These students are among those who remember their library as the safe place they so desperately needed.

However, going against the prevailing conventions means these books are the ones that are most frequently challenged or banned. Because of that reality, librarians sometimes pause before ordering a book with an LGBTQ+ character. In some communities, there is a high risk of the title being challenged.

But if the librarian is afraid to purchase it, think of the LGBTQ+ student in your school who must live with that fear every day.

Facing a book challenge is frightening, but the right to read and free access to information are what librarians stand for. Should you find yourself in this situation, ALA's Office for Intellectual Freedom (www.ala.org/oif) offers help and will send letters of support. Your state library association will do so as well. Librarians have dealt with this on many topics over the years. It takes conviction and courage.

Only you will know whether you decided not to purchase a book because you were afraid of a possible challenge. The ethics of our profession say you should make that purchase, but the choice is ultimately yours. Consider your philosophy, mission, and vision when you make it.

All libraries should have a board-approved selection policy that includes a procedure to follow when a book is challenged. If you don't have one, work with other librarians in the district to write one. Chapter 11 goes into detail on how to create one using ALA's Selection and Retention Policy Toolkit (www .ala.org/tools/challengesupport/selectionpolicytoolkit).

Special Needs Students

Special needs students are a part of every school, but they may not feel as though they are. It's mirrors and windows again. By definition these include physical, developmental, and emotional disabilities. Students in regular classes need to see them as people, and special needs students need others to see them for who they are, rather than seeing only their disabilities. Your collection should include books that feature special needs kids.

When the needs of the student can be managed in a traditional class, schools use inclusion to foster that understanding. These students may have aides to help them when necessary. You can use the aide's experience to make sure these students are truly a part of your class. Some special needs students do not have an aide but will have an Individualized Education Program (IEP). Students with certain special needs, as specified by the Individuals with Disabilities Education Act (IDEA), have a legal right to a special plan written by a multidisciplinary team. The IEP sets learning goals for these students and states the services the school district will provide. After a series of tests and observations determine the child's need for an IEP, a team (generally including a special education teacher, a classroom teacher, a building principal, a psychologist, and the child's parents or guardians) designs a program of services to blend the best methods of teaching with the most conducive learning environment for the child.

The process of creating the IEP allows the parties to discuss and resolve any differences of opinions and needs. The document specifies the decision-making process and anticipated outcomes, and it includes the child's current level of educational performance, specific services to be provided, the person who will provide those services and when they will do so, the amount of time the child will be in regular and special classrooms, and short- and long-term goals. The IEP objectives are used to determine the child's progress toward the goals. A well-written, carefully developed IEP protects the child because schools are legally responsible for implementing it.

The challenge for you is that you are also responsible for implementing IEPs, but you probably won't be told which students them have unless you ask. Speak with guidance counselors and classroom teachers to be sure you understand students' limits and the best ways for working with them.

Students may also have a 504 Plan. This ensures that there are accommodations in place to meet the students' needs. This sounds very similar to an IEP, but there are differences. For example, a student with a physical disability may not need to have individual educational goals set, but the district must make necessary accommodations to facilities.

Check with teachers to learn which, if any, of their students have IEPs and 504 Plans. You are responsible for following it.

English Language Learners

English Language Learners (ELLs) are often in special classes until they become more proficient in English. Many librarians have found that ELL teachers are the most willing to collaborate with them.

The range of reading levels and books with pictures make your collection ideal for improving ELL students' language skills. They will often gravitate to the library and to you. If you are at the high school level, you may want to get some easy chapter books or picture books from the elementary librarian but be careful that you are not insulting any students. Graphic novels can also help.

As you work with these students, remember that their difficulties with mastering the English language has nothing to do with their intellectual abilities. There is a tendency to treat ELL students as though they are less intelligent. They are as capable of learning research skills as your other students. They just need to be able to access material that is at their current English language reading level.

For all these and all your other students, bring diversity into their learning experiences using the *National School Library Standards*. The Key Commitment for Shared Foundation II, Include, is "demonstrates an understanding of and commitment to inclusiveness and respect for the diversity in the learning community."[12] The Key Commitment for Shared Foundation IV, Curate, is "make meaning for oneself and others by collecting, organizing, and sharing resources of personal relevance."[13] As the librarian, you make this possible by curating a collection that represents diversity in all its forms with particular attention to the demographics of your school

David E. Robinson developed the "School Library Diversity Model and Assessment Guide."[14] It is only seven pages long. It will serve you well in analyzing yourself and your collection. It also can be incorporated into a portfolio you share with your administrators.

PRIVACY AND CONFIDENTIALITY

In a world where privacy is fast disappearing, you should protect students' privacy as much as possible. There are three federal laws regarding minors' privacy with which you should be familiar:

- *The Family Educational Rights and Privacy Act* (FERPA) gives parents certain rights with respect to their children's education records. These rights transfer to the student when they reach the age of eighteen or attend a school beyond the high school level. Students to whom the rights have transferred are "eligible students." [15]
- *The Children's Online Privacy Protection Act* (COPPA) "imposes certain requirements on operators of websites or online services directed to children under thirteen years of age, and on operators of other websites or online services that have actual knowledge that they are collecting personal information online from a child under thirteen years of age." [16]
- *The Protection of Pupil Rights Amendment* (PPRA) affords certain rights to parents of minor students with regard to surveys that ask questions of a personal nature. Briefly, the law requires that schools obtain written consent from parents before minor students are required to participate in any U.S. Department of Education funded survey, analysis, or evaluation that reveals information concerning eight areas. [17]

Make sure your automated system is not maintaining a history of what students borrowed. You only need information about what they have currently checked out. When sending overdue notices to teachers, make separate sheets for each student, staple it closed, and put the student's name on the outside. Another possibility would be to have your system send overdue e-mails to students. You can let teachers know which students have overdues, and they can tell them to check at the library.

Anyone who works in the library and checks books out, whether a clerk or an adult or student volunteer, must know they are not to discuss students' reading interests outside of the library. They also should not discuss students' behavior with others. What happens in the library stays in the library.

Books that are not returned at the end of the year present a special problem. You should make a list of all outstanding materials; this is generally given to the school secretary, who will manage over the summer. Avoid the practice of posting the lists on the glass wall of the office waiting area. There is no reason for everyone to be able to see who borrowed what.

Because students are minors, their parents do have a right to know what their child is reading. Assuming your system does not keep a borrowing history, you can only let them know what is currently checked out. You must also comply if a parent asks you to restrict their child from reading certain books.

Parents sometimes request that books they find objectional be removed from the library. That is outside their rights. They can't decide what other children read. Respond calmly. If they demand titles be removed, begin to follow the procedure defined in your selection and reconsideration policy.

ALA has a web page on privacy that provides numerous resources to guide you in protecting student privacy.[18] Its link to the ALA Privacy Toolkit (www .ala.org/advocacy/privacy/toolkit) on that page will help you to draft your own privacy policy. It is particularly important to be familiar with the Library Privacy Guidelines for K–12 Students. There is also a page of links on students and minors at ALA's *Choose Privacy Every Day* blog (https://chooseprivacy everyday.org/).

Your automated library system can be another place where student privacy is violated. The Library Privacy Guidelines for Library Management Systems (www.ala.org/advocacy/privacy/guidelines/library-management-systems) let you know if any of its functions violate privacy. Make sure yours is compliant.

In addition to your automated system, your digital content vendors may be collecting information that violates student privacy. The Library Privacy Guidelines for E-Book Lending and Digital Content Vendors (www.ala.org/ advocacy/privacy/checklists/ebook-digital-content) covers the various areas where they may be collecting patron data.

A web page on Edsby.com titled "Avoiding Pitfalls in Student Data Privacy" lists questions to ask your different vendors.[19] The final question, "Is there a recovery plan in the case of a disaster?" has become extremely relevant in a world of ransomware that can take down the entire district. The site also reviews the red flags that should alert you when there is a possibility that your students' data may be compromised.

It seems like there are an overwhelming amount of resources and information on the subject, but all types of libraries are committed to protecting user privacy. Armed with these resources, you can demonstrate how you are guarding students' rights. You might want to discuss this with your administrators and the tech department, who may not be as aware of vendors' use of student information.

🔖 KEY IDEAS

- To be a safe, welcoming space, the library collection must reflect the many differences among the school population as well as the larger world.
- Differences go beyond race, culture, and ethnicity to include lifestyles, socioeconomic conditions, and physical and other disabilities.
- The library's selection policy must pay attention to equality, diversity, and inclusion (EDI).
- Equality is giving everyone the same thing. Equity is giving what is needed to level the playing field.
- Diversity encompasses an ever-increasing awareness of our many differences.
- Make sure your library is compliant with ADA.
- Inclusion means that all are part of the whole.
- To promote EDI your collection should have "mirrors," "windows," and "sliding glass doors," so that all students can see themselves and their lives in the library's resources as well as be able to see others' lives.
- Many of the materials dealing with diversity in the library's collection will deal with food, fashion, festivals, and folklore that give only a partial "window."
- The paucity of books on different cultures and ethnicity is a challenge to building a diverse collection, which should include books that are written by those from those cultures and ethnicity.
- A diverse collection develops tolerance and prepares students to be global citizens.
- Become aware of the gender spectrum and make adjustments to your language.
- Know the pronouns your LGBTQ+ students prefer.
- The decision to purchase a book with an LGBTQ+ character can be difficult as it may be challenged.
- All libraries need a selection and retention policy. The ALA Selection and Retention Policy Toolkit is a detailed guide on how to write one.
- Special needs students will have an Individualized Education Plan that sets goals for them and indicates what the district will provide.
- Some special need students have 504 Plans stipulating accommodations that will be made for them.
- Speak with teachers to learn if any of their students have such plans.

- Have books and other resources for English Language Learners but recognize their language and reading difficulties do not indicate any intellectual deficiency.
- Libraries should put in place a privacy policy to protect students' rights.
- Be familiar with FERPA, COPPA, and PPRA.
- Students' borrowing histories should be private. However, parents are permitted access.
- In addition to ensuring your automated system vendor is not accessing students' data, also check to be sure your digital content vendors are also compliant.

NOTES

1. U.S. Census Bureau, "Quick Facts," 2018, https://www.census.gov/quickfacts/fact/table/US/PST045218.
2. ADA National Network, "What Is the Americans with Disabilities Act (ADA)?" 2019, https://adata.org/learn-about-ada.
3. Sedley Abercrombie, "Making a Library More Accessible for Students with Special Needs," *Knowledge Quest* (blog), November 22, 2017, https://knowledgequest.aasl.org/making-school-library-accessible-students-special-needs/.
4. American Association of School Librarians, *National School Library Standards for Learners, School Librarians, and School Libraries*, 2018, 75–82.
5. AASL, *National School Library Standards*, 93–102.
6. American Library Association, "Equity, Diversity, and Inclusion," *Intersections*, www.ala.org/advocacy/diversity.
7. American Library Association, "Diversity: An Interpretation of the Library Bill of Rights," 2019, www.ala.org/advocacy/intfreedom/librarybill/interpretations/diversecollections.
8. Rudine Sims Bishop, "Mirrors, Windows, and Sliding Glass Doors," *Reading Is Fundamental*, 2015, https://scenicregional.org/wp-content/uploads/2017/08/Mirrors-Windows-and-Sliding-Glass-Doors.pdf.
9. Jamie Campbell Naidoo, *The Importance of Diversity in Library Programs and Material Collections for Children*, Association for Library Services to Children, 2014, www.ala.org/alsc/sites/ala.org.alsc/files/content/ALSCwhitepaper_importance%20of%20diversity_with%20graphics_FINAL.pdf.
10. Cooperative Children's Book Center, "The #OwnVoices Gap in African-American Children's Books," *CCBlogC*, 2017, http://ccblogc.blogspot.com/2017/03/the-ownvoices-gap-in-african-american.html.
11. Anthony Ciuffo, "Rethinking Conventions: Keeping Gender-Diverse Students Safe," *Educational Leadership*, October 2019, 70–75.
12. AASL, *National School Library Standards*, 76–77.
13. AASL, *National School Library Standards*, 94–95.

14. David E. Robinson, "School Library Diversity Model and Assessment Guide," *Knowledge Quest,* November/ December 2019, https://knowledgequest.aasl.org/wp-content/uploads/2019/10/KNOW_48_2_OE_Robinson.pdf.

15. U.S. Department of Education, https://www2.ed.gov/policy/gen/guid/fpco/ferpa/index.html *Family Educational Rights and Privacy Act* (FERPA).

16. Federal Trade Commission, *Children's Online Privacy Protection Act* (COPPA), https://www.ftc.gov/enforcement/rules/rulemaking-regulatory-reform-proceedings/childrens-online-privacy-protection-rule.

17. U.S. Department of Education "Laws and Guidance General: PPRA for Parents," https://www2.ed.gov/policy/gen/guid/fpco/ppra/parents.html.

18. American Library Association, "Privacy," April 2017, www.ala.org/advocacy/privacy.

19. "Avoiding Pitfalls in Student Data Privacy," *Edsby,* September 26, 2019, https://www.edsby.com/student-data-privacy/?d25ck=70&i25ck=6NtU4&s25ck=SmartBrief+student+data+privacy+article+...+%28Click+Campaign%29&x25ck=230.

9
Assessments

Assessments and evaluations are part of life. We make these decisions whether we are buying a car or choosing a place to eat dinner. But when the assessments are about us and our own performance, there is always some anxiety—and perhaps even fear.

Students have always dreaded tests and report cards. We know that high-stakes tests have caused them so much stress that some schools are adding yoga and calming rooms to help them cope. The library should be a place where students don't feel judged. However, you do need to assess the success of the lesson.

You need to know what was learned. How well did the lesson go? Evaluations are necessary for improvement. You can't fix anything if you don't know what didn't go well. Just because you taught something doesn't mean it was learned.

A variety of assessment tools allow you to keep track of how students are doing and make necessary adjustments. Just as students, we also do not like being judged. It is hard to discover your lesson went over kids' heads or bored them silly because they already knew the material, but you need the information to improve your program and your teaching.

Although it is upsetting to learn that a lesson you taught missed the mark, it is even harder to face assessments from administrators. There have always been formal assessments such as the observations and end-of-year reviews, but today you also have to deal with weightier mandated evaluations. These evaluation instruments tend to cause you the most stress, but they are manageable once you become familiar with them.

Don't overlook the importance of informal self-assessment. You use them with students all the time. You can do the same with your own performance. Along with research-based assessments that you construct, you are able to provide data to add value to the formal ones.

STUDENT ASSESSMENTS

In addition to the discussion in chapter 3 about student assessment, it is helpful to focus on the range and purpose of different assessments. You recognize that assessing learning is imperative, but what methods should be used, and when? In this instance you and the classroom teachers have the same goals. You both need to make assessments an integral part of your lessons.

Formative and summative assessments are what we most often rely on. Formative assessments let you and the students know how you are all doing during the course of a project. It serves as feedback. Summative assessment shows what was learned.

Pre-Assessment

Before you do formative and summative assessments, you might also want to incorporate some diagnostic or pre-assessment as a first step. The most common pre-assessment tool is having students do a KWL chart. The "K," which stands for "what I KNOW," forms the pre-assessment. The "W," for "what I WANT to know," sets the direction. "L," for "what I LEARNED," is a simple summative assessment.

Pre-assessment is vital for differentiating instruction. It lets you know the range of knowledge students will bring to a project so that you can give them tasks at their level. Depending on what you are doing, students may have different aspects of the subject to explore, or you can set up stations appropriate to where students are. Emily Pendergrass describes how to do this in her article, "Differentiation: It Starts with Pre-Assessment."[1]

You may have used an entry ticket or asked a question verbally to focus students on the upcoming lesson. It can also be used as a pre-assessment For example, if you were going to do a unit on gardening because students are starting one for the school, you might ask them to tell you:

- One thing I know about gardening is …
- Two garden tools are….
- The most important thing to remember when gardening is….

You can ask the same questions as exit tickets, which will serve as an informal summative assessment that demonstrates what the students have learned.

Formative Assessment

Formative assessment is the most helpful form of assessment for you and students. The object of teaching is learning, not "gotcha." Formative assessment allows time to make changes and helps students learn to do this on their own. To ensure that no one is left behind, use an assortment of formative assessment techniques such as the ones discussed below.

Good teachers and librarians pay close attention to students' faces. Blank expressions, perplexed looks, or eyes focused elsewhere are instant indicators that you are not getting through. They're signals to pause and have students restate what was covered before resuming.

Many librarians use the "thumb" technique." Thumb up—I completely understand. Thumb to the side—I am unsure, still working on this. Thumb down—I am lost. Brief, ungraded quizzes are another technique.

These are some of the more common formative assessments:

- *Think/pair/share*. Ask a question that requires understanding, not just a restatement, of what you are teaching. Give students a few minutes to write out their answers. Have them discuss their answer with another student. If you wish, you can have them report back with a summary of the pair's answer.
- *3-2-1*. A variation of this is sometimes used with exit tickets. After class, ask students to write three things they didn't know before, two things they found interesting, and one thing they want to explore further.
- *Red, green cards*. Give students a card with green on one side and red on the other. When they are understanding the lesson, they show the green card. As soon as they are confused, they raise the red card, which is your signal to stop, find out what is causing the confusion, and then explain it better. You can do this with red and yellow cards, with yellow indicating uncertainty. If there are several yellows, stop.
- *Four corners*. This incorporates physical motion into the lesson. Prepare a few questions, each of which has four possible answers. Use four areas of the library reasonably close to where you are teaching. Each area represents one of the answers. Students move to the spot for the answer they believe is correct. (You can also use this as a final summative evaluation.)

- *Journaling.* Have students reflect on their learning. (You can decide if you want to collect and read them.) Alternatively, ask them to use their journals to formulate questions about what they want more information about and leave them with you. (You can also have them ask these questions in class.

For more formative assessment ideas see the Squarehead Teachers website for a downloadable PDF chart with a variety of formative assessments.[2] You can also use technology for formative assessments. Kahoot (https://kahoot.com/) allows you to create multiple choice questions in the form of games. It's available as an app or through a web browser. For older students, Quizlet (https://quizlet.com/), which is also available in both formats lets you create flash cards and other learning tools. Also check AASL's Best Digital Tools for Teaching and Learning (www.ala.org/aasl/awards/best).

Formative assessment should be regarded as feedback, not criticism. When you are not getting the results you want, formative assessment lets you know in time to make changes. Although disappointing, not getting it right the first time is not a failure. This is the message you've been urging your students to take to heart—and so should you. The same formative assessment can inform both students and you.

I once worked with a general science teacher on a project dealing with recycling and composting. I had presented a lesson using databases where the kids got to work in groups to search for information. I thought I had done well and wouldn't have given it another thought. "Job done," I thought. How much they hadn't learned surfaced when students gave preliminary oral reports in which they only included general knowledge but missed significant ideas because they had not found the most relevant resources. The class hadn't learned what I thought I'd taught. Students were creating Google searches that didn't focus on key concepts.

Fortunately, I had a good relationship with the teacher, so they felt comfortable in letting me know how disappointed they were with the results. We decided to bring the class back to the library for a follow-up lesson. We discussed "scientific" terms, the importance of determining what was relevant to the topic, and how to better frame their searches. I also reviewed helpful databases. Both the teacher and I made a bigger point of monitoring where students were searching.

This was the first time they had done the unit with me in the library, and I was grateful for the second chance. The results were impressive. The teacher and the students were pleased. We repeated the unit the next year, confirming that the mistakes were not repeated and making additional modifications. The results were even better.

Ideally, as you incorporate formative assessments into your lessons, students learn to self-evaluate. By knowing when to try a different approach or ask for help, they are prepared for their journey as lifelong learners.

Summative Assessment

Summative assessments look at results. In education, as in the real world, these are what count. It's the unit test, and it's the stress-inducing high-stakes tests. Although the district looks at the latter to make changes for the future, the unfortunate truth is there is no mechanism for a do-over.. If the summative evaluation shows that students didn't learn a concept, there's a hole in their education that may cause a problem later.

Summative evaluations don't need to be elaborate. Framing your exit ticket questions carefully can give you a good picture of what was learned and what wasn't. Because you can't fix it now, make notes about what was missed. Next time you teach it you will be able to make the necessary changes. (Save the tickets to show your administrator what students learned.)

Another alternative is a Twitter board. Give students small sheets of paper. Have them write what they learned using Twitter's text limits, either the original 140 or the newer 280 characters. Post their tweets on a board. Encourage them to add a hashtag.

While these two examples are simple, summative assessments are usually big projects as they are meant to demonstrate how much was learned. Students may prepare a slide presentation, create an infographic, or design a product to meet a need. If you worked with a classroom teacher on the learning experience, try to arrange for students give their presentations in the library or go to the classroom to observe them. By seeing the final product, you will have your own summative evaluation. What did kids do well? Where could it have been better? What was the quality of their sources?

Assessment of students is generally associated with grades. Elementary librarians usually must give grades for report cards. This is unfortunate because the library should be the one place in the school where students are not judged.

You can mitigate the problem by giving grades based on student dispositions rather than products. For example, assess how well students follow directions, their ability to collaborate effectively, and their persistence in dealing with research.

On the other hand, as noted in chapter 6, some middle and high school students may be disrespectful and disruptive because they don't see you as their teacher and you don't give them grades. The suggestion there was to grade their "Works Cited" pages. Although you still are not recording a grade on their report cards, this will help you to become more important in students' minds and makes them more likely to come to you for advice on sources.

SELF-ASSESSMENTS FOR AND BY THE SCHOOL LIBRARIAN

Your program and your work within it will also be assessed. In addition to the reviews given at district and state levels, you should conduct a self-assessment. This obviously will look at student learning, but your focus is on identifying holes in your teaching and improving your practice.

You have learned the results of your teaching through the formative and summative assessments you used with students, but there are also more formal ways to get this information that tend to carry more weight. Find out the results of high-stakes tests. See where the data shows students are weak. It is possible you can address it as part of your library program. Communicate this to your principal. Demonstrating your contribution to school goals raises your value to the administration.

Action Research

Another method of gathering information is to conduct an action research project to document your work. Richard Sagor's book for ASCD, *Guiding School Improvement with Action Research*, explains when and how to do this and how the results should be used.[3] The first chapter is available online and gives a good overview of what it is and the components of action research. It identifies the following seven steps:

1. Selecting a focus
2. Clarifying theories
3. Identifying research questions
4. Collecting data
5. Analyzing data
6. Reporting results
7. Taking informed action

Eileen Ferrance has written an approachable booklet on action research that is a guide for conducting an action research project.[4] Her list of steps is similar to Sagor's but emphasizes the cyclic intent of action research:

- Identify the problem.
- Gather data.
- Interpret data.
- Act on evidence.
- Evaluate results.
- Next steps.

And then you are back to identifying the problem.

As you prepare to implement action research, identify a significant problem. As with an essential question, it should not be a yes or no question. You will be investing a lot of effort into this. You want it to be meaningful to you—and to your administrators.

Both Sagor and Ferrance give examples of what kinds of data might be collected. For example, you can use surveys, student portfolios and journals, or the results from a high-stakes test. It depends on the problem you are looking at.

Although you can analyze the data on your own simply by reviewing it, if you plan to discuss the results with your administrator, use a more formal way of documenting it. Based on what you have discovered, revise or change what you are doing. Then reassess to see if it worked.

The real challenge is to find the time to do all this. It is one thing for a school to implement a continuous cycle of action research, but it's another for the librarian to incorporate it into their busy schedule. Although action research is supposed to be continuous, this may be more than you can handle.

Before teaching the lesson, obtain the number of searches conducted in the database in the course of one month. The first time you try an action research project, work with something relatively small, for example, teaching students how to use specific databases to encourage them to use sources other than Google or YouTube. Check the number of uses after you have taught the lesson and students do a project.

Even if you decide action research would be a valuable assessment tool for your program, you may throw up your hands at the time commitment involved. One alternative is to connect with a nearby graduate school of education. A doctoral candidate or a professor might very well be glad for the opportunity to conduct such a research project. Not only will you get the benefit of their professional expertise, you will also increase the credibility of the findings you present to the administration. As a bonus, this work might also be publishable.

Evidence-Based Practice

Somewhat similar to action research, evidence-based practice (EBP) is also cyclic and produces hard data to evaluate and improve your program. It originated in medicine but has been embraced by school librarianship.

EBP seeks to meld research into the daily practice of librarians. Too often research is done in isolation from what a librarian is facing every day. School librarians may read the results of the research but do not necessarily implement the findings. To accomplish this, EBP uses three approaches. Judi Moreillon's article in *Knowledge Quest* succinctly explained them as follows:[5]

- *Evidence for practice* uses research to guide decision-making regarding the process of instruction. Find articles and books and incorporate the information when developing lesson plans and classroom management strategies.
- *Evidence in practice* involves collecting locally generated data during the teaching and learning process. Assess students' outputs (e.g., understanding of the content and processes of their learning) based on what you have taught.

- *Evidence of practice* includes reflecting on student outcomes, sharing results with stakeholders, and using evidence to guide subsequent instructional decisions.

You can see how helpful it is to identify formative assessments that can lead to developing evidenced-based practices (and how similar this is to action research). Administrators who aren't necessarily interested in data from studies done in other locations will look more seriously at those done in your school with your students.

ASSESSMENTS OF THE SCHOOL LIBRARIAN

Teaching classes is only one of your many roles and responsibilities, yet that may be the only aspect of your job on which you are assessed. It begins with formal observations. Typically, your principal or supervisor will observe you teaching a class. In most situations, this will be written up as though you were a classroom teacher.

However, you don't have the continuity classroom teachers have. Even in elementary schools where you have a fixed schedule, you see students at best once a week. Although your lesson may not be directly connected to the previous one, you are always building on what came before. This requires you to help students recall any key concepts they will need for the current lesson. When you have your post-observation conference, address when and why you did this. It will give your principal more of an idea of what you do and how your work is different from the classroom teachers.

It is even more challenging at the middle and high school levels, where your teaching is based on any collaborative lessons you have scheduled. Most commonly, your supervisor or the principal's secretary will ask when you are next teaching. In addition to providing your lesson plan, prepare a brief summary of how the lesson fits in to what has preceded it, where it is going, and what the ultimate outcomes are. Don't just reference the letter of the Domain and the Roman numeral of the Shared Foundation. Spell out the most significant standards you will be addressing,

Use the post-observation conference to subtly show how your teaching affects student achievement. At all levels, be prepared to respond to any criticism included in the observation. Couch your rebuttal as "clarification."

You might also suggest an observation based on your other responsibilities. It would be a short conference during which you would review your collaborative and cooperative work with teachers, technology integration, new projects, and the like. The principal would then evaluate that work and determine if it aligns with your job description beyond your teaching.

In a number of states teachers must submit Student Growth Outcomes (SGO) or Student Learning Outcomes (SLO) at the start of the school year during which they will be assessed. Librarians are not always required to do these, but it's a good idea to know how they are done and prepare one to reinforce your end-of-year evaluation.

In general, you need to select a meaningful outcome that reflects learning as a whole. It should be measurable, have data to support the results, and it should be realistic. You certainly don't want to set yourself up for failure.

Like action research, EBP can provide you with the data you need to show learner outcomes. If librarians are required to write EBPs in a number of districts, the state library association usually has some sample ones on their website. Use them as a template for constructing your own.

Annual Assessments

At the end of the year your principal or supervisor will assess your performance. If you were required to submit an SGO or SLO it will be evaluated at this time. Use this time wisely. You can subtly inform your administrator about your responsibilities and accomplishments.

Many librarians complain that their administrators don't know what they do. It is your job to inform them. Send your message via quarterly reports— whether required or not—using web resources such as Piktochart (https:// piktochart.com/) or Canva (https://canva.com). The combination of text and visuals is best for getting your point across.

Even if you can't manage a quarterly report, an annual report is a must. Again, use a web-based resource that allows you to incorporate pictures and videos. In addition, submit a "brag sheet" summing up any activities your principal might not know about. Include any district committees you are on and attendance at workshops and state and national conferences, along with what you learned, and if you presented at these conferences.

For your use and for sharing with your administrators, I recommend you print out the evaluation checklists from AASL's *National School Library Standards* (https://standards.aasl.org/project/evaluation/). If you are enterprising, have them printed on card stock and laminate, or purchase them. Share with your administrator to show what a highly effective school librarian does.

Most school districts these days use a formal instrument to standardize the end-of-year assessment process. The most common one used is the Danielson Evaluation Instrument.[6] Although is over eighty pages, you can scan it quickly to get the gist of it.

The instrument evaluates teachers in four domains:

- Planning and Preparation
- The Classroom Environment
- Instruction
- Professional Responsibilities

There are numerous criteria within each domain, and you are rated on a scale of 1 to 4 with "1" being "Unsatisfactory" and "4" being "Distinguished." From what I understand, the "4" rating is not given often. The best you may get is a "3" for "Proficient."

This is an excellent instrument, but it is designed for teachers—and teaching is not the sum of what you do. Most districts currently do use it for school librarians, which is a cause for frustration. What makes it even more so is that Danielson has also created a framework for library media specialists.[7]

This framework also has four domains.

- Planning and Preparation
- The Environment
- Delivery of Service
- Professional Responsibilities

The differences between the two frameworks are more obvious when you examine what is assessed under each. For example, Component 1a under Planning and Preparation is "Demonstrating knowledge of literature and current trends in library/media practice and information technology."

It is unfortunate that this framework for school librarians is not more widely used. Principals may think that using a different instrument requires too much extra work. It requires the librarian to provide artifacts to demonstrate evidence for each of the domains. Lawrence Township (New Jersey) has excellent examples of supporting artifacts on its library webpage. For example, artifacts for supporting that first assessment under Component 1a are

> samples of e-mails to staff with new library materials; an article from a library periodical and/or a PLN with examples of how this new idea was incorporated into your library program; a link to your Goodreads page; your book order; reports from your circulation system detailing how you improved deficient areas in your collection; examples of student/staff requests and evidence of filling those requests.[8]

You might use such artifacts in a discussion with administrators when encouraging them to use the library media specialist framework instead of the one for teachers. Artifacts are also helpful when you write your end-of-year report.

The Georgia Library Media Association has developed the School Library Evaluation Instrument (SLEI), which is aligned with the *National School Library Standards*.[9] It includes guidance for the evaluator and uses ten performance indicators. The list of indicators speaks to the wide range of the librarian's responsibilities:

1. Instructional Partner
2. Role of Reading
3. Informational and Technology Literacy

4. Instructional Leadership
5. Effective Practices for Research
6. Program Planning and Administration
7. Positive Learning Environment
8. Collection Development
9. Professionalism and Communication

A definition is given for each performance indicator followed by examples of how they might be demonstrated. For "instructional partner," the school librarian's responsibilities are:

- Meets with teachers and administrators on a regular basis to collaboratively develop plans that are clear, logical, sequential, and integrated.
- Collaborates to provide flexible, consistent, and personalized approaches to academic content to align and connect the research process and information literacy skills to the state or local standards and student needs.
- Assesses student understanding and progress throughout learning activities by asking questions, observing works-in-progress, evaluating artifacts of learning, and communicating with teachers.
- Chooses and recommends print and online resources that support instruction and the identified needs of diverse learners.

The school librarian is then rated on the scale of Levels I through IV. Level III is the expected level and IV is going above and beyond.

The Marzano Focused Teacher Evaluation Model is another assessment used nationally. It is standards-based, uses formative assessments, and focuses on student results. The model measures teacher effectiveness using twenty-three essential behaviors to measure teacher effectiveness in four areas of expertise. The four domains are:

1. Standards-Based Planning (three elements)
2. Standards-Based Instruction (ten elements)
3. Conditions for Learning (seven elements),
4. Professional Responsibilities (three elements) [10]

All elements are scored throughout the school year rather than at the end. The goal is help teachers improve their practice through the feedback as they are evaluated.

New York State's *NYSED School Library Media Program Evaluation Rubric* is another comprehensive evaluation instrument.[11] It divides the evaluation into three large areas: teaching for learning, building the learning environment, and empowering learning through leadership. There is also a section on action planning.

An introduction to each area gives explanatory guidelines taken from the last iteration of the AASL standards. For example, Teaching for Learning lists:

1. The school library media program promotes collaboration among members of the learning community and encourages learners to be independent, lifelong users and producers of ideas and information.
2. The school library media program promotes reading as a foundational skill for learning, personal growth, and enjoyment.
3. The school library media program provides instruction that addresses multiple literacies, including information literacy, media literacy, visual literacy, and technology literacy.
4. The school library media program models an inquiry-based approach to learning and the information search process.
5. The school library media program is guided by regular assessment of student learning to ensure the program is meeting its goals.[12]

Additionally, the three areas are further subdivided into a total of twenty-five elements. The ten under Teaching for Learning are:

- Instructional Design
- Collaborative Planning
- Informational Literacy
- Reading
- Assessment for Learning
- Teaching for Diverse Learning Needs
- Inquiry Learning
- Intellectual Freedom
- Social Learning
- Social Responsibility[13]

There are explanations of what each section entails, what it looks like in practice, and additional relevant links.

Although you only need to be familiar with the evaluation instrument your administrator will use, being aware of these other evaluations helps to give you a deeper understanding of what a school librarian should be doing. You may be constrained by time and budget, but this shows what you are aiming for.

Be proactive in communicating to your administrator what you do and how it contributes to student achievement. Make an appointment to meet during the summer when their schedule is less hectic. As part of your discussion , share the evaluation instruments you feel best describe the range of what you are trying to accomplish.

🔢 KEY IDEAS

- We are always making assessments. It's what helps us make decisions.
- Assessments are needed in order to make improvements.
- High-stakes tests for students and evaluation instruments for you cause the most stress.
- Formative assessment provides feedback so that changes can be made while learning is taking place.
- Use a variety of simple formative assessments to determine whether students are following the lesson or getting lost.
- Kahoot and Quizlet are two tech tools that can produce formative assessments.
- Check AASL's *Best Digital Tools for Teaching and Learning and Best Digital Tools*.
- Summative assessments look at results and include presentations, projects, and tests.
- Summative assessments guide the future because they assess instruction that is already completed
- For less weighty formative assessments use exit tickets or a Twitter board.
- Your principal will likely evaluate you several times a year by coming in to observe as you teach a lesson.
- Provide the principal with background information indicating what the lesson being evaluated is based on and where it is going.
- Suggest an evaluation "conference" with your principal to cover your non-teaching responsibilities.
- Action research is a, multi-evaluation method to improve the quality of your teaching; ideally, it is conducted cyclically.
- After identifying a significant problem area, collect data.
- If analyzing the data seems too complex to handle on your own, consider working with a graduate student from a nearby college.
- Implement your findings and assess whether the revisions worked. Share the information with your administrator.
- Evidenced-based practice (EBP) uses research to make changes in how you design and teach lessons.
- The three aspects of EBP are:
  - *Evidence for practice*. Articles and books on research.
  - *Evidence in practice*. Using the research in teaching.
  - *Evidence of practice*. Reflecting on the results of implementing the research-based practice.
- Your state may require you to submit student learning outcomes (SLO) or student growth outcomes (SGO) as an evaluation instrument for your year's work.

- Check your state library association's website for sample SLOs or SGOs to use as a template for creating your own.
- Consider developing an SLO or SGO even if you are not required to use either in documenting your work for your end-of-year evaluation.
- Quarterly reports are good for keeping administrators informed, but you must also submit an annual report.
- Use a web resource that integrates text, pictures, and video to make your report more interesting.
- Share the AASL evaluation checklists with your principal.
- Submit a "brag sheet" to your administrator in advance of your end-of-year evaluation to inform them about activities they may not be aware of.
- Most states are now using a formal evaluation instrument.
- The Danielson Evaluation Instrument is the most commonly used assessment, but there are others.
- If the Danielson teacher evaluation is used, you most likely will be evaluated as a teacher even though there is a Danielson evaluation for school librarians.
- You will need "artifacts" to demonstrate your work as a school librarian.
- The Georgia Library Media Association has developed an evaluation instrument based on the *National School Library Standards* that assess librarians in nine areas giving performance indicators for all of them.
- The Marzano Focused Teacher Evaluation Model assesses teacher effectiveness in twenty-three elements divided into four domains throughout the year.
- The New York State Education Department has an evaluation instrument divided in to three areas, which are further subdivided into twenty-five elements.
- These evaluation instruments can help broaden your understanding of what you should be aiming for and can be used in a discussion with your administrator.

NOTES

1. Emily Pendergrass, "Differentiation: It Starts with Pre-Assessment," *Educational Leadership* 71, no. 4 (December 2013/January 2014), www.ascd.org/publications/educational_leadership/dec13/vol71/num04/Differentiation@_It_Starts_with_Pre-Assessment.aspx.
2. "Quick and Easy Formative Assessments," *Squarehead Teachers*, https://squareheadteachers.files.wordpress.com/2012/09/formative-assessments.pdf.

3. Richard Sagor, "Guiding School Improvement with Action Research," ASCD, 2000, www.ascd.org/publications/books/100047/chapters/What-Is-Action-Research%C2%A2.aspx.

4. Eileen Ferrance, "Themes in Education: Action Research," LAB: Northeastern and Islands Regional Laboratory at Brown University, 2000, https://www.brown.edu/academics/education-alliance/sites/brown.edu.academics.education-alliance/files/publications/act_research.pdf.

5. Judi Moreillon, "Reading and the Library Program: An Expanded Role for the Twenty-First Century SLMS," *Knowledge Quest* 38 (2), 24–31.

6. Charlotte Danielson, *Danielson Evaluation Instrument,* 2013, www.loccsd.ca/~div15/wp-content/uploads/2015/09/2013-framework-for-teaching-evaluation-instrument.pdf.

7. Charlotte Danielson, *Danielson Framework—Library Media Specialists,* https://www.wwps.org/images/departments/personnel/Evaluation_Process/Library_Media_Framework.pdf.

8. Wendy Offery, April Oliver, Michele Casieri, Gabrielle Immordino, and Mary Silagy, *Danielson Sample Artifacts for Evidence in the Library Media Center*, LMS Library Media Center, https://sites.google.com/a/ltps.info/lms-library-media-center/teachers/danielson-sample-evidence-library-media.

9. Georgia Library Media Association, *School Librarian Evaluation Instrument*, 2018, https://www.glma-inc.org/slei

10. Beverley Carbaugh, Robert Marzano, and, Michael Toth, *The Marzano Focused Teacher Evaluation Model: A Focused, Scientific-Behavioral Evaluation Model for Standards- Based Classrooms* (West Palm Beach, FL: Learning Sciences International, 2017), 9, https://www.learningsciences.com/wp/wp-content/uploads/2017/06/Focus-Eval-Model-Overview-2017.pdf.

11. New York State Education Department, *NYSED School Library Media Program Evaluation Rubric,* www.nysed.gov/school-library-services/nysed-school-library-media-program-evaluation-rubric.

12. Georgia Library Media Association.

13. Georgia Library Media Association.

10
Ending the Year Right

Wrapping up the year right is as important as getting off to a good start. You certainly don't want to return to unresolved problems next year. The challenge is to get everything done while still dealing with your classroom responsibilities and other tasks.

APPROACHING THE FINISH LINE

You will need to have a discussion with your principal about closing dates. If you are an elementary librarian, you will continue meeting with your classes until the last day of school. At the middle and high school levels, it is common to stop teaching classes about two weeks before that. Teachers often do not want to be involved in research projects that late in the year, but some teachers may want to bring a class in to finish an assignment.

You have a myriad of tasks to complete before the school year ends. When you are new to a position, this can feel overwhelming. (It's a heavy load even if you aren't new.) To avoid being swamped, make a list of what you are required to do and plan how you will manage it.

Teen Services Underground has created a school library year-end check-list that covers most of your responsibilities.[1] You are likely to discover there are others as you go along. Just add them to your list.

Collecting Books

Your big job will be getting all outstanding materials back. Even as you begin the process, start work on putting the shelves in order. It will help considerably when kids claim that they returned their books.

Although you send overdue notices throughout the year, it becomes critical now. Send reminders to students about returning books and post a reminder sign by your checkout desk. Unreturned materials are recorded as still being in circulation as they are during the year, but with a summer intervening getting them back becomes more difficult.

Remember to safeguard students' privacy when sending these overdue notices. Some elementary librarians inform parents via e-mail. In most places it's legal for parents to know what their young children are reading (there are different rules for "older minors"). Some states, like New York (see New York Consolidated Laws, Civil Practice Law and Rules—CVP § 4509) are stricter about it, making it a challenge to get the books. At the upper grades the e-mail often goes directly to students.

Many of you still send paper notices. If you do, put the homeroom number and student name on the outside of a folded sheet of paper and list the titles on the inside, then staple it closed. Teachers should not know what books students have checked out.

Lost books are a problem that non-librarians don't think about. You may not charge fines, but most libraries will require payment for lost books. How should you handle that? Should you use a flat fee depending on year of publication? And there's a dirty little secret—any monies collected go to the board of education, so you won't have the funds to replace the book.

Incentives help students to return their books. Some librarians offer small prizes such as bookmarks when a student has returned all their books. Elementary and middle school librarians can hold competitions to see which class has a clean slate. If the administration supports it, students who haven't returned their books can be barred from participating in year-end activities such as field days. Some schools hold up report cards, although that may run into legal issues.

One elementary librarian dressed up as a robot (i.e., **R**eturn **O**ur **B**ooks **O**n **T**ime) and visited classrooms. The first class to have zero overdues won a pizza party, and the rest of the classes that had no overdues had popsicle parties.

Many schools schedule a locker clean-out time. Try to be present for this. Buried in the lockers are many oft-forgotten books. Bring a book truck with you. You will need it.

In some middle and high schools, an administrator will accompany staff who open lockers to search for missing books. To respect students' privacy, a better alternative is to send the students to open their lockers and search for books. You will be amazed at how many turn up. If you do charge fines (although it's best not to), you can figure out how much students owe when you check the books in.

Despite your best efforts, there will be students who don't return their books. Although these will be marked as lost, you still want to get them back. At many schools, at the end of the school year the librarian prepares a list organized by grade or teacher that gives the names of the students and the titles they haven't returned. The school secretary handles the list and any returns or payments for lost books during the summer.

This practice is problematic. As we discussed in chapter 8, students have a right to privacy. To make it worse, some schools post the end-of-year list on the glass panels of the general office. That should never be done.

Optimally, the list given to the secretary should only contain the students' names and the number of books checked out. The titles should only be listed and sent in separate envelopes addressed to the student. . This is a great deal of work. You might just give the secretary the list with the titles, although it does violate student privacy.

In addition to getting books back from students, you also need to get them back from teachers, which can require some diplomacy. Some teachers will want to keep them until just about the last day. Work with the vendor of your library management system. If you are doing summer loans, go into the classroom, mark books there as returned, and then check them out for the summer.

Summer Loans

Most of you have an automated systems in which you entered your closing date for circulation at the start of the school year. However, give some thought to allowing books to be borrowed for summer reading. Librarians are doing this increasingly often because they recognize students can't always go to the public library or afford to buy books. As one librarian noted, "Why would I keep books from kids when they have the most time to read?"

Summer circulation can be a one-time checkout for the whole summer with the due date set for when school reopens. Alternatively, the library can remain open during the summer. for a day or two a week, only once a month or just for an evening family night. Students usually can borrow up to ten books at a time, although some allow this only with parental consent. Determine who will staff the library

You will lose a few books, whether you have summer loan just before school ends or keep the library open some days during summer, but this isn't much different from losses incurred during the school year. Another benefit of having the library open during the summer is that it's a powerful advocacy statement that shows how the library is valued. At the elementary level, parents will come with their children and see the library firsthand.

One important caveat. If you are going to do this, you need approval from the administration. Who will be responsible for opening and closing the library? Will access to the rest of the building need to be closed off? What costs are involved? Will custodians have to work extra? Will you get a stipend?

Inventory

Not every librarian does a yearly inventory, and some only do partials. Your districts may or may not require one. But if you don't do a regular inventory, your OPAC (or card catalog) will not be an accurate reflection of your holdings.

The School Library Media Specialist has an article on inventorying the library collection. It briefly explains what it is, why it's necessary, what should be inventoried, and who should be involved. It's a good way to ground yourself before you begin.[2]

If you are doing a year-end inventory, whether full or partial, you need the time to complete it. Your automated system vendor will help you set it up and provide directions. It is time-intensive even with automation. For those of you who still have a card catalog, it's even more so. In either case, you can't do it while you are teaching classes. The tight schedule means many librarians come in after the school year to complete the inventory even if they aren't paid. This is where volunteers are extremely helpful. Even if you stop teaching before school ends, volunteers can make the job go much faster. They also can begin the process while you are still working with classes.

Adult or student volunteers show their worth here; however, regardless of whether you use Dewey or a genrefied system, you will have to train them. Even regular library users are not always attuned to the subtleties of the many subdivisions. If you put books in series in sequence rather than title order, they need to know that as well.

As books are returned, some shelves become tight. Optimally shelves should be one-half to three-quarters full, so this necessitates shelf-shifting, which is another time-consuming task. Once they understand the process, volunteers can handle the job, although it can become a bit tricky when the bottom shelf of a bookcase at the end of an aisle is full and books must be shifted to the next aisle.

The inventory process with a library automated system consists of scanning the barcode of each book. You need as many scanners as you have people working. Sometimes you can borrow scanners from another school in the district that's not doing an inventory at this time.

Time-intensive as it is, automation is a tremendous improvement over the old paper system, where you worked with a card shelf list to identify what should be on the shelf. If it was there, you turned the book down. If it wasn't there you turned the card up. And if you found a book without a record, you left it standing. At the end of the inventory, the standing books needed to be pulled and records found or made, the turned-down books had to be stood up again, and the shelf list had to be marked showing the book as lost.

With an automated system, you generate a printout of what is lost. Books that are still overdue are considered as being in the collection. The system will mark the year it was not located on the shelf. You need to decide at what point to delete the title from the collection. You don't want to replace it immediately because it might turn up. If you do delete it, should you reorder it, assuming it's still in print?

Many librarians are also responsible for inventorying textbooks. It very well may be one more job you have to complete as you wrap up the school year. Find out if you must do this in your school. You don't want to discover this has to be done just as you think you have finished. Your automated system can do this the same way it does with your library collection. If this function hasn't been previously set up, contact your vendor for help.

Weeding

Weeding is necessary to keep the collection up to date. That said, it can be fraught with anxiety, frustration, and even anger. Important as weeding is, there are some librarians who are resistant to it.

Optimally, weeding should be ongoing throughout the year. Removing books that are outdated, contain misinformation, or need repair is vital to maintaining and building a collection that meets the needs of students and teachers. Old titles clutter your shelves, making it difficult to find current ones, and they give your library a dated look. Think of it as pruning—removing what doesn't contribute to give the rest room to grow.

During the year, you can pull books as you come across them and delete them from the collection. You can also focus on a section that needs updating. Inventory and book return give you another opportunity to get more weeding done.

Before you begin weeding, be prepared for blowback. Teachers, custodial staff who might see books in the trash, and volunteers are often upset that you are getting rid of books. It seems counterintuitive to what a librarian should do.

Make a list of the reasons why you weed. Send them out in a newsletter, post it on your website or on any social media you use. Hannah Byrd Little's two-part series on weeding without controversy gives advice on why it's necessary to weed and how to do it. The first part, "Why Weed?" suggests ways to avoid, or at least minimize, the controversy and presents a strategy for getting the job done.[3] The second part looks at the process itself and offers suggestion for how to go about it.[4]

You can set up a display of "howlers." Somehow, no matter how regularly you weed, some titles slip through. These examples of truly outdated books or those that are in bad physical shape can quietly explain why weeding is important.

In a short time, you will have amassed a number of books to discard. Now what? Should you just chuck them in a large garbage can? Give them away? You may not have a choice. Many districts have a procedure for discarding materials bought with taxpayer money. Check with your administrator to find out how you are supposed to handle this.

If there aren't any guidelines, you need to decide what to do with the discards. My favorite is to give them to art teachers to use in projects. Some librarians use them to make paper crafts for use in library displays.

My least favorite is giving them away. If the books are no longer suitable for your own students, why should they go to others? However, some librarians have book sales (which may not be allowed if the books were bought with taxpayer money) or use them as end-of-the-year giveaways.

Set parameters for what signals that a book that should be discarded. These should be included in a collection development policy that should be part of your selection and retention policy. The CREW method (which stands for Continuous Review, Evaluation, and Weeding) and the acronym MUSTIE (Musty, Ugly, Superseded, Trivial, Irrelevant, maybe obtained Elsewhere) are favorites among librarians. These are excellent guidelines for volunteers to follow.

The Texas State Library and Archives Commission has produced a manual on CREW, which includes a helpful PowerPoint presentation.[5] You might even share it with your volunteers and give them some responsibility for weeding.

For those of you who still don't like the thought of throwing away "perfectly good" books, think about what you are saying: "These books are in such bad shape, I don't want my students using them. But it's okay to give them to others." Or perhaps, "These books contain dated or misinformation, so I don't want my students using them. Less fortunate kids can use them." Stick to using the discards for art projects. If you want to help those without books, raise money for them.

Volunteers can put books they think should be weeded on a cart for you to review. If you determine a book still belongs in the library, explain why. It helps to expand volunteers' understanding as to why you might keep a book that seems to meet the parameters for weeding.

Weeding by volunteers will never be as complete as it would be if you were doing it, but considering the size of the task, it's a good trade-off.

Doing comprehensive weeding while you are simultaneously doing an inventory can be overwhelming. Instead, consider focusing on sections of the collection. Collection mapping will tell you which areas are most outdated,

The old method of collection mapping was to check the copyright date of every tenth book on the shelf. If a significant number of titles were earlier than the cut-off date you chose, that section would need weeding. Fortunately, you have a better option.

Even if you don't use Follett's Destiny library management system, you can use its Titlewave (www.titlewave.com) to do a collection mapping project. You need to give them a school e-mail address and then upload your collection. You will get back a beautiful report with graphs and other information detailing the age of each section of your collection. With the data in hand, you can begin weeding, and you'll have evidence to show your administration and others why you are doing so. All of you are likely to be surprised at the age of your collection.

Summer Work

Whether you do any work in the library over the summer is a personal decision. Obviously, if you are being paid for opening the library for summer circulation, you go in. You may be fortunate to be on a curriculum writing or mapping committee, in which case you are also being paid while you are integrating the school library program into the curriculum.

There are other reasons for going in. You may not have completed your inventory. As noted, it is hard to get it done while you are still meeting with classes. Having a blissfully quiet space makes the job go faster.

Many librarians go in for several hours a few times during the summer to attend to mail and perhaps even unpack books and other supplies that have arrived. Legally, you can wait until school starts, but you already know how hectic that time is. Go in if it is worth it to you to reduce the stress of opening the library.

You probably will set up your opening displays several days before you are officially supposed to report. The time available at the beginning of the school year in the one or two days before students start is never enough to get this done. While you are doing this, expect teachers to drop in with questions and requests. Although this takes time away from what you are doing, it's a good thing. It shows that teachers recognize your value and gives you some quiet time to build relationships.

If you have a union in your district, check in with one of its representatives. You may get blowback for coming in without getting paid, the argument being that if you do it for free, you will never get paid for it. (It's true, but you do need to decide whether the advance preparation makes your life easier.) Keep in mind that during contract negotiations, the union will be more forceful about doing work without getting paid. When that is the issue, you shouldn't go in. It will alienate you from the teachers.

Plan on coming in one day during the summer to meet with your principal. This is a quiet time for administrators, when they can focus on what you have to say without the distractions of their usual days. Use the time to discuss you plans and goals for the upcoming year.

Find out what the principal wants to achieve and suggest ways you can help. If you would like to put in a special request when you submit your budget for the next year, put forward your reasoning now. When CD-ROMs were the latest technology, I wanted to purchase a CD tower for $20,000, which then seemed like an enormous amount of money. I handled this by working with the superintendent. They asked what I was willing to cut. I made some tough decisions, which they accepted, and my budget request went through without a hitch.

REFLECTION AND GROWTH

Once the school year has ended, but before you ease into your summer break, make time to reflect on the past year. What have you learned about your teachers, students, and yourself? How have you grown as a librarian?

What projects were most successful? What made them so? What can you do to improve on them next year? What didn't work the way you intended? Why? Is there anything you can do differently, or should you try something else entirely new?

Review your mission and vision statements. Do they still say everything you want them to? If not, this is the time to tweak it. As you look at it, does it suggest a project you might undertake in the fall?

Consider taking on some new challenges. Take a critical look at your website. Compare it to those of other libraries. Does yours need a fresh look? If you don't have a website, now is the time to plan one. Contact your tech department to find out how to go about it.

Hopefully, you have broadened teachers' awareness of what students learn and do in the library classroom. If you submit quarterly and annual reports, your administration will begin to appreciate your role in the educational community and your contributions to student growth and achievement. But other stakeholders are also important.

Look for ways to let parents and the community know what happens in today's library. You can write a regular column for the school's newsletter or create one for the library. Find out if your local newspaper would be interested in featuring activities happening in the school library.

Catch up on your professional reading. Have you saved professional journals because you didn't have time to read them? You have time now. Select one or two ideas that appeal to you and plan to launch them next school year.

Consider taking a summer course or some webinars. There are a number of online courses. AASL's e-COLLAB (www.ala.org/aasl/ecollab) has several that are archived. There is some free content. Explore what is available and see what interests you. As a role model for lifelong learning, you need to continually expand your knowledge.

Next year's successes begin with how you spend your summer.

🔲 KEY IDEAS

- Although the end of the school year is hectic for everyone, it is even more so for school librarians.
- Set a final date for circulating material with the approval of your principal.
- Collecting outstanding and overdue material will be your main task.
- Put shelves in order to help in determining whether a book was actually returned.
- When sending overdue notices, be careful not to violate students' privacy.
- Some districts prevent students from participating in end-of-year activities or even hold their report cards if they haven't returned their books.
- Incentives help in getting books returned. They can range from giving out bookmarks to throwing a pizza party.
- Participate in locker cleanout because many books will be unearthed.
- You also need to get books back from teachers. Because they are harried, you may want to go into their rooms and get their permission to retrieve the books.
- There are many good reasons for lending books out over the summer.
- Decide whether summer loans will involve a single checkout of many books with returns when school resumes, or if the library will be open for circulations on several days throughout the summer.
- Get administrator approval and determine who will staff the library when it's open during the summer.
- Traditionally, whole or partial inventories are done at the end of the school year.
- Without an inventory, your OPAC or card catalog is not an accurate reflection of your collection.
- Inventory is time-intensive. If at all possible, get adult or student volunteers to help.
- Take time to train volunteers as they may not have a secure understanding of your shelf arrangement.
- The return of outstanding books may cause some shelves to become very tight, which will require shifting.
- Inform volunteers about the optimum amount of space that should be left on each shelf and how to move books to keep them in order. This is particularly necessary when they must be moved to another bookcase.

- In an automated system, each barcoded item must be scanned.
- You need a scanner for each volunteer.
- You may be able to borrow scanners from other schools in the district if they aren't doing an inventory at this time.
- Find out if you are also responsible for inventorying textbooks. If you are, it should be done through your automated system.
- Weeding is necessary to keep the collection current.
- Optimally, weeding should be done throughout the year.
- Additional weeding naturally occurs during inventory and book collection.
- Many in the school are upset when they discover the library is discarding books.
- Even some librarians are resistant to weeding.
- To minimize blowback, be proactive. Let everyone know you are weeding and why.
- Set up a display of howlers—books that are obviously in need of weeding.
- Find out if your district has a procedure for discarding materials bought with taxpayer money.
- If there is no procedure, decide what to do.
- My favorite is to use the books for art projects or give them to the art teacher to do the same.
- My least favorite is to give them away. If they are not good enough for your students, why would they be good for someone else?
- Set clear parameters for what should be discarded.
- The CREW method and MUSTIE are commonly used.
- Have volunteers put the books they think are ready for discard on a cart for you to review. Explain why you decide to keep any of those titles.
- To limit the extent of end of year weeding, map the collection to find the sections that are most outdated. Titlewave by Follett will let you do this for free.
- Donating books you have discarded because they are in bad shape, outdated, or contain misinformation sends the message that although they are not suitable for your students they are fine for those who are less fortunate.
- Other than jobs for which you are paid, whether or not to work during the summer is your decision.
- Reasons for working in the summer may include completing the inventory, unpacking deliveries to the library, and going through the mail.
- Do come in a day or so before your scheduled start time to set up opening displays.

- Plan on a meeting with your principal over the summer to discuss your goals for the upcoming year and to learn their plans so you can help to achieve them.
- Begin your summer vacation by reflecting on the past school year.
- Review your mission and vision statements to assess whether they should be tweaked.
- Evaluate your website to see if it needs to be updated.
- If you don't have a website, contact your tech department to learn how to set one up.
- Reach out to your community. Consider writing about library activities for a local newspaper.
- Catch up on professional reading and give thought to taking a course or some webinars.

NOTES

1. Sereena Hamm, "School Library Year-End Checklist," *Teen Services Underground,* May 20, 2016, https://www.teenservicesunderground.com/school-library-year-end-checklist/.
2. "Library Media Program: Inventory," *The School Library Media Specialist,* https://eduscapes.com/sms/program/inventory.html.
3. Hannah Byrd Little, "Weeding Without Controversy: Part One—Why Weed?" *Knowledge Quest* (blog) March 12, 2019, https://knowledgequest.aasl.org/weeding-without-controversy-part-one-why-weed/.
4. Hannah Byrd Little, "Weeding Without Controversy: Part Two—The Process," *Knowledge Quest* (blog), April 2, 2019, https://knowledgequest.aasl.org/weeding-without-controversy-part-two-the-process/.
5. Texas State Library and Archives Commission, *CREW: A Weeding Manual for School Libraries,* 2018, https://www.tsl.texas.gov/ld/pubs/crew/index.html.

11
Managing the Whole

Having brought the school year to a close, you might think there is nothing more to do. But as the past chapters have shown, there is always more. Managing the school library classroom as well as how it extends into your full program is complex and consists of many facets.

What remains to be considered are plans, guidelines, and policies that cover the many aspects of your job. Some have been touched on in previous chapters as they relate to specific topics. Here they are gathered in one place.

You don't need to create them all at once, but some have higher priorities. Each gives you a strong basis for your decisions and actions. You should have guidelines that cover circulation of materials, an acceptable use policy (AUP); a selection and retention policy, which incorporates a number of other policies; and a privacy policy.

There is an important difference between policies and guidelines. Librarians often use the term *policy* when referring to what is technically a guideline. Policies require board of education approval. Guidelines are what you create to formalize your operating procedures. Policies carry legal weight. Guidelines don't.

CIRCULATION GUIDELINES

Circulation guidelines are a case in point. Although these are frequently referred to as policies, they are rarely board-approved. Many librarians don't have anything formal. Far too many circulation guidelines just follow procedures that have become habit.

A circulation guideline covers how many books students may borrow, how long, they can check them out, and whether renewals are allowed. It lists what the fines are for overdue books and whether students can borrow books if they have overdues, as well as how charges are set for lost or damaged materials.

Many current circulation guidelines are based on precedents established long ago and may need to be reconsidered to reflect today's world. Libraries have always charged fines and historically have not permitted students to borrow more books if they have outstanding loans. This sounds logical, but many have come to appreciate that fines can work against our current philosophy.

More and more school and public librarians have taken a closer look at fines. As a result, they have changed their rules. It's worth thinking about the messages your circulation guidelines send and how they can impact student learning and students' love of libraries and books. Fines can be a barrier to use for students. This is contrary to your philosophy of the library as a safe, welcoming environment. Students living in poverty are often afraid to borrow books when they know they can't afford to pay fines. A lost book could be a serious problem.

There are many reasons students return their books late. Some split time between their divorced parents and may leave things in one parent's home, which means they aren't available when a student leaves for school from the other parent's home. They can't get the book until they are back with the first parent.

Others have even more complicated home lives. There is more homelessness than we may know. When there is no fixed residence, locating a book can be a challenge. When there is violence or addiction in the home, things are easily misplaced. Chapter 6 discussed ACE and the need for trauma-informed learning. Because these children badly need the "mirrors" you have in your collection, it would be a shame to deprive them of books.

Your circulation guidelines should also deal with charges for lost or damaged books. You might stipulate that if a book is over five years old, there is a flat fee. For more current titles you need to decide whether to charge the cost of replacing the book or a flat fee. Be aware that you are unlikely to be given any of the money you collect to replace the items. It usually goes to the school board. You might completely dispense with having students pay for lost books and develop guidelines that allow them to work off their fines by volunteering in the library. This procedure should apply to everyone, not just for the students who can't afford to pay.

There is a tendency among librarians to worry about lost books. The library is your responsibility, so it is natural for you to be concerned about lost books. This is why some librarians don't want to allow summer loans. Looking at it another way puts it into perspective. If you didn't allow books to circulate at all, you wouldn't lose any. (Although you probably lose some to theft). In the Middle Ages, books were chained to the shelf. No books ever got lost. But we know that when books are used, they can get damaged or lost. It's a fact of life and a cost of doing business.

Many school librarians don't permit a student to borrow a book if they have one that is overdue. They feel this teaches students responsibility. Yes, you want the books back, but the message you are sending is that learning about responsibility is more important than reading. Is this more important than creating a safe, welcoming space?

Once you complete your circulation guidelines, run them by your principal. Even though they won't become a board-approved policy, administrators don't like to be blindsided. Someone might complain to the principal about one of your "rules," so it's best that that they are aware of them. This also gives you a chance to explain your reasoning about the guidelines and how it promotes reading.

CLASSROOM MANAGEMENT PLANS

Many teachers have classroom management plans, but librarians tend not to create them. Although doing so takes time, having a plan in place will not only serve you. It also can be shared with administrators to help them have a better understanding of what you do.

Your plan should have the following components:

- Your philosophy of teaching and learning
- Your guidelines for the library environment
    - Facility considerations such as the arrangement and height of bookcases, seating, teaching, and display areas
    - How much noise is allowed? Indicate how you will let students know what is acceptable and when.
    - Rules about behavior in the library. How will these be established? Will there by consequences?

- Routines you will establish for running the library
- Guidelines for transitions and interactions with students in class
    - What techniques will you use to move students from one activity to another?
    - How will you engage them?
    - How will you deal with defiant behavior?

- Guidelines for interactions with others
  - Teachers
  - Students who are not in the class you are teaching
  - Volunteers
  - Administrators and any of their guests
  - Anticipated challenges and how you will deal with them

Through the OER Commons, you can access The IRIS Center at Vanderbilt University's two-part module on classroom management. Part 1 focuses on the components of the plan.[1] Part 2 covers developing your own plan.[2]

Erin Norris, a student in my Classroom Management for School Librarians course constructed a comprehensive classroom management plan using the above guidelines. She added her library's mission and vision statements, which is a good idea as you will submit your plan to the administration. She saved time by adapting material from Teachers Pay Teachers (https://www.teacherspayteachers.com/) and other online sources for considerations such as noise levels and rules and expectations.

As one small part of her plan, Norris identified the following methods of positive reinforcement:

- *Secret student.* Tell the class that you are observing a certain student who is behaving appropriately. Write the name of that student on a piece of paper. At the end of the class period, you reveal the name of the student. If the secret student is well-behaved, they earn a reward. Occasionally you may switch the name if a student who usually is not well-behaved displays good behavior during the observation period.
- *Award chart.* Make a chart of each class in grid form. Create boxes for each day a class is in the library. Put a sticker in a box for that week if the class was well-behaved. If the class earns a certain number of stickers, the class will get a special reward.
- *Raffle tickets.* Hand out raffle tickets for good behavior. At the end of class, hold a drawing and reward the student who has the winning ticket.
- *Watch a movie.* This can be an alternative to having a lesson.
- *Read outside.* This will of course depend on the weather.
- *Take out an extra book.*
- *Draw from a prize bucket.*
- Get a bookmark or pencil.

Most importantly, Norris developed an action plan outlining how the classroom management plan was to be put into operation, including starting and completion dates for each part.

ACCEPTABLE USE POLICIES

Acceptable use policies (AUPs) are always board-approved and apply through-out the district. An AUP spells out what behaviors are permitted or prohibited in using the district's technology. It defines rights and responsibilities. It also specifies consequences for violating the rules.

Although the AUP is for district-wide use, the librarian is the one most often responsible for its administration. Before students can use any digital resources, they must have a parent or guardian review the policy and sign off on its contents. The librarian is often the one who collects and files the returned agreements.

Violations of the AUP are more likely to occur in the library because students are doing research and working on computers. In 1:1 schools infractions also occur in other areas. However, you are responsible for what happens in the library. You need to know what procedures you are to follow when you see students violating the AUP.

Rapid changes in technology mean the AUP should be updated regularly. For example, an older policy may not address the use of social media. It is wise to schedule review of the policy every three or four years to ensure revision is not overlooked. A committee generally works with the IT department on the updates. Try to be part of that committee so you know what changes to expect.

When you read through the AUP, note whether it might come across negatively. As with your rules and expectations, it should have a positive tone and explain why appropriate use of all digital tools is important. If you are on the committee rewriting the AUP, suggest it stress how the students benefit from the district's technology.

The *Education World* website offers good information on how to get started creating an AUP.[3] Although the article hasn't been updated since 2009, it is sufficiently generic to get you started. The one thing it doesn't address is identifying consequences for violating the policy. You don't always have to state these in absolute terms because leeway is sometimes necessary, but students should know there are consequences for misbehavior.[4]

Two AUPs from different districts illustrate different approaches to the policy. The Corcoran Unified School District (California) has an extensive policy incorporating tools such as Google docs.[5] As you might expect, the document is fairly long, running five pages. The number of items it covers is an excellent example of why AUPs need frequent updating.

By contrast, the policy of Burlington High School (Georgia) policy is only about one page.[6] In the unlikely case that you don't have an existing policy, you might want to start with a simple policy like this to get one in place as soon as possible. You can then work on developing a more extensive one.

COLLECTION DEVELOPMENT PLAN

A collection development plan is an important part of the selection and development policy. In reality, few school librarians have a written collection development plan. And in times of tight or nonexistent budgets, it hardly seems necessary.

Is a collection development plan important? It certainly isn't vital, but it is worth thinking about. It can improve your decision-making.

Consider the purpose of your collection. How well does it meet that purpose? What changes need to be made?

A LIS 6101 blog post on collection development policies (or in our case, plans, as school librarians are not likely to submit this for board approval) quotes the ALA definition: "documents which define the scope of a library's existing collections, plan for the continuing development of resources, identify collection strengths, and outline the relationship between selection philosophy and the institution's goals, general selection criteria, and intellectual freedom."[7]

The blog post lists the elements of the plan, again drawn from ALA. I have listed here only those that are relevant to school libraries.

- introduction
- general purpose
- brief note about the library
- types of materials collected
- format of materials collected
- special collections

I have omitted weeding and deselection. Important as that process is, it belongs in the selection and retention policy. Indeed, you can include this plan in that policy to make it more formal and legal.

If you do write a collection development plan, share it with your administrator. Most likely they have no idea what is involved, what informs the choices you make, and the range of resources you evaluate when making purchasing decisions.

SELECTION AND RETENTION POLICY

Every library—school, public, and academic—should have a board-approved selection and retention policy. Unfortunately, few do, and, given the contentious nature of these times, it is more important than ever. It is a legal protection for you and the school board.

The policy explains how you acquire materials (so it covers a lot of what is in a collection development plan). It should give guidelines detailing when materials should be deselected or weeded, which can help to stem some of the criticism you may hear from those who don't understand the purpose of weeding. Also included are the procedures and any options for what to do with discarded materials.

A selection and retention policy goes far beyond what is in a collection development policy. It also deals with challenged materials and includes procedures for reconsideration of materials. It is an extensive document. Fortunately, you don't have to create it on your own. ALA's Selection and Reconsideration Toolkit for Public, School, and Academic Libraries covers each aspect of such a policy and provides suggestions and wording for all of them.[8]

Go through the Selection and Reconsideration Toolkit to familiarize yourself with its structure and contents. Because it will be a district-wide policy, you need to work on it with all the other district librarians. Time is at a premium for all of you, so you might want to assign the different parts and create a shared Google doc where everyone can work. You can then review what each of you has done. You are free to copy-paste directly from this toolkit and make changes where appropriate.

The following will go through sections of the Selection and Reconsideration Toolkit for Public, School, and Academic Libraries and discuss how they relate to the school library. (Links to the different sections are at www.ala.org/tools/challengesupport/selectionpolicytoolkit).

Basic Components

Mission Statement. Basic Components begins with a mission statement. While you have one in place for your own library, this is when you will want to write one for the district library program.

Support for Intellectual Freedom. You will probably want to incorporate the text that pertains to school library from Support for Intellectual Freedom:

> **Example: School Library Support for Intellectual Freedom**
> The school libraries of this district are guided by the principles set forth in the Library Bill of Rights and its interpretative statements, including "Access to Resources and Services in the School Library Program" and The Students' Right to Read statement of the National Council of Teachers of English. See Appendix (in this policy) for the Library Bill of Rights, "Access to Resources and Services in the School Library Program," and The Students' Right to Read statement. (www.ala.org/tools/challengesupport/selectionpolicytoolkit/intellectualfreedom)

Note the documents referenced include Access to Resources and Services in the School Library Program and the Students' Right to Read statement of the National Council of Teachers of English.

Objectives. All four of the sample objectives for school libraries are worth including.

Responsibility for Selection. Although you are the one responsible for making the selection of materials, note the wording that is given in the toolkit. It recognizes the legal role of the school board and superintendent of schools, but also emphasizes that "responsibility for actual selection rests with professionally trained library personnel."

Selection Criteria. Eleven selection criteria are given. These include representing different viewpoints on controversial issues and promoting diversity by having resources by authors and producers of all cultures. This section recognizes selection goes beyond books to the various multimedia sources that are now needed in a quality collection.

Acquisition Procedures. This section addresses purchase recommendations from "administrators, teachers, students, district personnel, and community members." You may not feel the need to include a section addressing this in your policy. However, if you do have any special collections in your library it should be part of the policy.

Selecting Controversial Materials. On the other hand, you definitely want to include a section on this. It is a brief statement. It begins "The school board subscribes to the principles expressed in the American Library Association's Library Bill of Rights. This makes the board of education compliant with the First Amendment and supports you and your program when someone challenges a library resource.

In chapter 8, we discussed the importance of "mirrors," that is, books and resources that mirror students' worlds. Often these titles are controversial, dealing with LGBTQ+ stories. The ALA list of the ten most challenged books of the year increasingly has a larger percentage being challenged because of LGBTQ+ themes.[9]

Gifts and Donations. Unless you receive gifts and donations, you may want to omit this section. However, include this if you want to ensure that you aren't pressured to accept a book or magazines (*National Geographic* used to be a frequent donation). It helps you deal with parents who gift you with items they want to discard and want a valuation for tax purposes.

Collection Maintenance and Weeding. This is where you could put a collection development plan. This section of the toolkit is not as detailed as what was discussed in the collection development plan, but it does spell out the reason and importance for weeding. You will probably want to make a decision about whether you wish to commit to an annual inventory. It's important to do it regularly but you can do half your collection one year and the rest the following year or have a continuous weeding plan. The cycle would be up to you.

Policy Revision. This acts as a reminder not to "file and forget." Your selection and retention policy should be reviewed regularly. You want to remove what is outdated and add new material formats if it is necessary to specify them. As an aside, when you get a new administrator, and they turn over rapidly in these days, be sure to tell them about the Policy.

Reconsideration

Although the other components of the toolkit are important, the one you will rely on if there is a challenge is the procedure for reconsideration. When you are faced with a challenge, no matter how prepared you are, you will experience a moment of panic and fear. With a policy in place, you can quickly calm down, and follow the board-approved steps.

Guiding Principles. These set the framework for how the challenge is to be handled. The first of the nine bulleted points clearly and briefly defines what is included in a library, stating, "Libraries have diverse materials reflecting differing points of view, and a library's mission is to provide access to information to all users." Equally important from the perspective of "what happens now?" is: "Questioned items will remain in circulation during the reconsideration process." Other points address that the item is to be considered in its entirety.

Statement of Policy. The example is brief, and you may include it as written.

Informal Complaints. Most of the challenges school librarians face fall into this category. Someone comes to you with a concern about a library resource. After a discussion, the issue is dropped. Sometimes a parent is satisfied knowing their child can be kept from the material to which they object. In other cases, they understand your explanation of why the resource was purchased and the purpose it serves.

Because there is no follow-up action, you might not consider it a challenge. But it was. It's important that you report it to ALA (www.ala.org/tools/challengesupport/report) because it keeps track of what materials are being challenged. ALA wants information about challenges for its annual list of most challenged books. (Recently there have been challenges to databases, too.) To remain on top of the issue and be prepared to give you support, ALA needs to know what is happening throughout the country.

Formal Reconsideration. This is the procedure you invoke when the person making the challenge wants the resource removed. The toolkit lists sixteen procedures, each with numbered steps, starting with the complaint going to the principal. Following the second step, "A concerned citizen who is dissatisfied with earlier informal discussions will be offered a packet of materials which includes the library's mission statement, selection policy, request for reconsideration of instructional resources form, and the Library Bill of Rights," may lead to a complaint being dropped.

In the event that it isn't, the next steps go through the issue being sent up to increasingly higher levels of reconsideration committees, beginning at the school level and ending with the board of education. The toolkit provides a sample School Library Request for Reconsideration of Material Form that requires the complainant to be specific about their reasons for making the challenge. Also included is a School Library Sample Letter to Person Requesting Reconsideration, which is the cover letter for the packet of information the complainant receives.

Reconsideration Committees. The section completes the toolkit. It lists best practices for committee members and repeats that challenged material should not be removed while the reconsideration process is under way. A Sample Reconsideration Committee Report illustrates how to bring the procedure to a close.

An appendix provides additional documents and resources.

A challenge is a grueling time for the school librarian. ALA's Office for Intellectual Freedom (www.ala.org/oif), your state school library association, and other national associations including the Intellectual Freedom Center of the National Conference for Teachers of English (www2.ncte.org/resources/ncte-intellectual-freedom-center/) are there to help you through it, but it will still be difficult.

For more detailed information, see "The Challenge of Book Challenges," a LibGuide prepared by Martha Hickson.[10] It was used during a panel presentation at the New Jersey Association of School Librarians. It is a tale of a very serious challenge and how it was successfully handled by a courageous and highly organized librarian. Its challenge tips and challenge toolkit are invaluable.

PRIVACY POLICY

Privacy is fast disappearing in our world, but as librarians we are responsible for protecting the privacy of our users. Privacy is a vital component to making the library a safe, welcoming space. Students pursuing topics of personal interest that may be on controversial subjects, may be afraid to borrow certain books for fear someone will find out.

As previously discussed, you need to ensure that overdue notices don't infringe on students' privacy rights. If you have volunteers working in the library, particularly adults, they must be informed of students' privacy rights. Make it clear they are not to discuss student borrowing –or behavior—outside of the library. And if they are checking students out, they should be careful of any comments they might make about the student's choice.

Libraries should not maintain a history of patron borrowing. Normally, that is the default setting on automated systems—confirm if yours is set that way. If someone in authority asks about a particular student's borrowing history, you can honestly say you have no data on that. Other incursions into student privacy may come from vendors collecting data as part of usage statistics. Before purchasing a database or other resource that has student inputting information, be sure to check the privacy policy.

A well-thought-out, board-approved privacy policy sets the guidelines for ensuring that users' privacy is protected. ALA's Library Policy in a Digital Age: Guidelines for Minors and Students in K–12 Schools collates all relevant ALA documents on the topic in one place along with links to additional resources.[11]

Review the ALA Guidelines for Students in K–12 Schools to familiarize yourself about data sharing and encryption along with what to include in a privacy audit.[12] The ALA Library Checklist for Students in K–12 Schools lists actions to take on three privacy priorities.[13] The Kent School District Library Media Program's FERPA guidelines" and Helen Adams's "School Library Privacy Checklist" will be helpful for creating your own privacy policy.[14]

ADVOCACY

We know that the librarian's role in managing the school library classroom is different from a classroom teacher's. One of the greatest differences is in the need and importance of advocacy. Teachers seldom have to advocate for their positions within their schools and districts. Librarians must.

Administrators and legislators are often unaware of how the school librarian impacts student achievement, how the librarian as tech integrator makes teachers more successful, and how they prepare students to be global citizens who will be producers as well as consumers of information. There are many reasons they do not recognize the importance of school librarians, much of which is based on the experiences they have had in the past.

In order to change those misconceptions, school librarians must actively promote their programs. It is your job to keep administrators informed of what is happening in the library. Brief quarterly reports incorporating pictures and videos showing students at work are most effective. If you can't make the time to do this every quarter, do an annual report—whether or not it's required.

Advocacy has two aspects. One is legislative. AASL works with ALA's Public Policy and Advocacy Office to lobby for legislation that strengthens libraries, including school libraries. Your state association does the same. The second is getting the word out about your library program.

The AASL website's section on advocacy (www.ala.org/aasl/advocacy) provides a wealth of resources. The section on legislation gives up-to-date information on what is happening on the national front. Resources include infographics, reports, and research and statistics. Of particular interest is its tools page (www.ala.org/aasl/advocacy/tools), where you will find downloadable brochures and posters. You'll also find a link to toolkits (www.ala.org/aasl/advocacy/tools/toolkits), which are extremely helpful. New ones are created as needed. The AASL Advocacy Toolkit: Educated Support for School Libraries and School Librarians and the Toolkit for Promoting School Libraries show how you can let all stakeholders know about the valuable contributions you and your library program make.

No matter how busy you are, you must always think about how to promote what you are doing. Never miss an opportunity to let everyone know that the library program—and you—are indispensable.

FINAL WORDS

We started out by looking at differences—between management and control, and between the classroom and the library classroom. We discussed how to create an atmosphere that sends the message that the library is a safe and welcoming space and then plunged into lesson plans designed for when you see different grades and subjects from one period to the next.

We explored the challenge of being responsible for multiple schools. We explored collaboration: how the librarian can collaborate with teachers and how to encourage students to collaborate with each other. You learned about personal learning networks (PLNs) that connect you to resources available to you from your colleagues and how to deal with or construct a library curriculum.

Highlighting the difference between the teacher's classroom and the library classroom, we looked at ways to handle the many disruptions that occur during your day and while you are teaching. Keeping the library orderly (not perfect, just orderly) involved shelving and time management.

You discovered that the library is used for many purposes in addition to teaching. Some are initiated by you, such as book fairs and author visits. Others are meetings and events set in the library, all of which you need to prepare for.

Always focusing on the importance of making the library a safe, welcoming environment for all, we explored what you must know about and do for minority and special needs students, as well as others who need to see themselves represented in the library.

We went over how the end of the school year requires a discussion on assessments for students and you, and reviewed the additional challenges posed by high-stakes tests. We reviewed standardized assessments where you may be evaluated as a teacher rather than a librarian.

Finally, we reviewed how to close the library—or not—at the end of the school year. We covered a lot of territory.

By now I hope you realize being a school librarian is a wonderful, exciting, and challenging job. It's like no other in the school. It takes skill and constant learning to manage it.

Did we cover it all? No. We did a lot, but there is always more. Technology, budgets, and political changes all impact the school library. Use your PLN and participate in national associations such as AASL to keep up.

🔲 KEY IDEAS

- Policies, guidelines, and plans give you formal justification for your decisions and actions.
- The board of education's approval is required for a document to be a policy.
- Circulation guidelines are often based on what has always been done.
- Charging fines for overdue books creates a financial barrier for many students.
- Books may be late because of difficult home situations.
- Reevaluate how you charge for lost or damaged books and if it makes sense to continue to do so.
- Not permitting students to borrow a book if they have overdues send the message that responsibility is more important than reading.
- Share your written circulation guidelines with your administrator and explain the reasoning behind them.
- A classroom management plan helps to manage your library teaching classroom as well as the rest of the library and serves as a communication tool with your principal.
- Your educational philosophy, routines, transitions, and interactions with others are among the components of the plan.
- Spell out the techniques you plan to use for positive reinforcement as well as how consequences are to be used.
- It is a good idea to include your mission and vision statements.
- Acceptable use policies (AUPs) are always board-approved.
- Although an AUP applies throughout the district, violations are most likely to occur in the library.
- With the rapid changes in technology, it is important to revise the AUP regularly.
- Volunteer to serve on the committee that revises the AUP.
- AUPs should set forth the benefits of using district resources and the reasons why ethical use of all digital resources is important.
- Collection development plans are not a requirement for school librarians, but the elements that go into them may help you be clearer on your purchasing decisions.
- Every library needs a selection and retention policy approved by the board of education.
- The ALA's Selection and Retention Policy Toolkit guides you through the process of writing a policy for your library.
- The basic components of the policy are mission, support for intellectual freedom, objectives, responsibility for selection,

selection criteria, acquisition procedures, special collections, selecting controversial materials, gifts and donations, collection maintenance and weeding, and policy revision.

- The reconsideration section of the policy explains the guiding principles, statement of policy, informal complaint, request for formal reconsideration, sample reconsideration form, sample letter to complainant, and reconsideration committees.
- An informal complaints is one that someone brings to the librarian or an administrator but is later dropped by the person who raised it.
- Informal complaints should be treated like challenges and be brought to ALA's Office for Intellectual Freedom.
- A LibGuide by Martha Hickson details the story of a particularly extensive challenge, which presents the details of what occurred, tips for dealing with challenges, and the appropriate toolkit to use.
- Librarians must safeguard users' privacy by keeping students' borrowing choices confidential, ensuring that vendors are not collecting personally identifiable data, and instructing any volunteers about student privacy rights.
- Librarians should create a privacy policy and seek to have it board-approved.
- Unlike teachers, school librarians must always be advocating for their program and looking for ways to communicate their message to all stakeholders.
- AASL's advocacy page has a wealth of material to help librarians get the word out.

NOTES

1. IRIS Center, "Classroom Management (Part 1): Learning the Components of a Comprehensive Behavior Management Plan," https://www.oercommons.org/courses/classroom-management-part-1-learning-the-components-of-a-comprehensive-behavior-management-planI.
2. IRIS Center, "Classroom Management (Part 2): Developing Your Own Comprehensive Behavior Management Plan," https://www.oercommons.org/courses/classroom-management-part-2-developing-your-own-comprehensive-behavior-mtoolkitanagement-plan/view.
3. "Getting Started on the Internet: Developing an Acceptable Use Policy (AUP)," *Education World,* 2009, https://www.educationworld.com/a_curr/curr093.shtml.
4. "K–12 Blueprint, Acceptable Use Policies: Focus on Student Learning," 2014, https://www.k12blueprint.com/sites/default/files/Acceptable-Use-Policies.pdf.

5. Corcoran Unified School District (California), "Acceptable Use Policy: For the Use of Computers, Mobile Devices, Internet Access, Google Apps for Educators Suite, and Internet Applications," 2011, http://swmcdn.com/site_0681/CUSD _AcceptableUsePolicy.pdf.

6. Burlington High School (Georgia), "Burlington High School Acceptable Use Policy," 2011, https://www.forsyth.k12.ga.us/Page/40831.

7. "Collection Development Policy," *LIS Blog,* 2009, http://lis6010blog.blogspot .com/2009/08/collection-development-policy.html .

8. American Library Association, Selection and Reconsideration Toolkit for Public, School, and Academic Libraries, 2018, www.ala.org/tools/challengesupport/ selectionpolicytoolkit.

9. American Library Association, "The Ten Most Challenged Book Lists," 2019, www.ala.org/advocacy/bbooks/frequentlychallengedbooks/top10.

10. Martha Hickson, "NJASL 2019: The Challenge of Book Challenges," North Hunterdon Library Media Center, http://libguides.nhvweb.net/c.php?g =973401&p=7036535.

11. American Library Association Office for Intellectual Freedom, Library Policy in a Digital Age: Guidelines for Minors and Students in K–12 Schools, https://drive .google.com/file/d/1DAdKeKNW18FpOKSy5wUtyljbyKHjPOM3/view.

12. American Library Association, Guidelines for Students in K–12 Schools, www.ala.org/advocacy/privacy/guidelines/students.

13. American Library Association, Library Checklist for Students for K–12 Schools, www.ala.org/advocacy/privacy/checklists/students.

14. Kent School District (Washington), Family Education Rights & Privacy Act (FERPA), https://www.kent.k12.wa.us/Page/10262; Helen Adams, "School Library Privacy Checklist," *Library Privacy in a Digital Age* (Chicago: ALA Office for Intellectual Freedom), https://americanlibrariesmagazine.org/wp-content/ uploads/2019/06/MinorsPrivacy2019.pdf.

Index